Poems from the Heart

Beatrice Wilson Crutchfield

First Edition

NEWMAN SPRINGS PUBLISHING
320 Broad Street
Red Bank, NJ 07701

First originally published by Newman Springs Publishing 2023

ISBN 979-8-88763-396-1 (Paperback)
ISBN 979-8-88763-398-5 (Hardcover)
ISBN 979-8-88763-397-8 (Digital)

Printed in the United States of America

To my loving family:

MY DAUGHTERS
Loreathea C. Fields and
Silvia C. Daniels
and their families

MY SON
Rucker Caesar Crutchfield, III
and his family

Contents

Acknowledgments

It was an honor and privilege for me to complete this book of poetry. My mother entrusted her poems to me because we were working on having them published before she passed away.

She had typed most of her poems. All I had to do was categorize them and put them into an electronic mode, so that they could be published.

It was truly a joy for me to read over her poems. She made me laugh and smile. There were times when I was in deep depression, but I began working on her poems, soon my depression was gone.

She often said that she could write poems in just a short period of time, which means to me that she was definitely gifted by God. During this time period, I learned of her innermost thoughts and rediscovered that she had a deep faith and belief in God. I'm so grateful to be able to share her poems with the world. She was truly a wonderfully, inspired person.

I give special thanks to my nephew-in-law, Brett Macias, who conducted a workshop which started me on this journey. Also, I would like to thank my daughter-in-law, Shirli Fields, my brother, Rucker Crutchfield, and my grandson, William Fields, III, who on Easter, 2021, helped me to realize that all of her poems were of great quality and none should be eliminated from this publication.

My daughter-in-law, Shirli, spent her precious time editing portions of this work. Thank you so much for your dedication.

To the new owners of this great publication, may you be as inspired as I was when I read these poems.

May God bless each of you.

Loreathea C. Fields

Advice

Steps Toward a Good Life

Live each minute fully day by day.
Put your very best in all you do. And try not to stray,
Far from the things you hoped to do.
Pick up loose ends and pieces that will help too.

Remember to put your best foot forward although there may be strife.
It's not an easy thing to do as you travel in this life.
Yet, that's what it takes to combat the challenges one meets.
Good, bad, and evil are many of the things we greet.

No one knows what to expect when he wakes up in the morn.
Surprises of all kinds are out there from the day you were born.
Although things are rough, they could be worse.
Look around the corner, there goes a hearse.

As long as life lasts, you can move further up.
When you are dead, you're done, and it's impossible to win the cup.
Remember the man you saw with no arms and legs.
He's still living although he may have to beg.

Count your blessings as you go on from day to day.
God will continue to bless you in His own special way.
Live your life happily, one day at a time.
Reach out to the Father, you'll hear the bells chime.

August 20, 1987

Give Your Best

You do not know what tomorrow will bring.
So live today fulfilling everything.
Give your best as you go along.
Be kind to others, you can't go wrong.

Help the poor and needy, you'll be blessed.
Give them strength and courage, God will do the rest.
Let your light shine in every way.
Piloting those who've gone astray.

Let your sails fly so high in the sky,
That they may be seen by a passerby.
He may need that bit of light,
To guide him safely thoroughly through the night.

Did you reach and touch somebody's hand today?
It might give him strength along the way.
God wants you to live so that all may see.
The Christ-like spirit imbedded in thee.

Lend a Helping Hand

Always try to lend a helping hand.
Then when you have problems others will understand.
You cannot live in this world by yourself.
Your problems and worries can't be put on a shelf.

Be good to your neighbor and to yourself be true.
Stand up for right, and you'll never be blue.
Be just in your dealings from day to day.
Then you'll have friends all along the way.

If you do all this, and things don't work out right.
Turn to the Master, always keep Him in sight.
He'll be a friend and neighbor too.
He'll protect and guide you and see you through.

Love One Another

They may laugh and talk behind your back.
But it behooves all of us to have more tact.
You never know what trials others may have to overcome.
Your time of need may be next for sympathy, so let's not be dumb.

People all have a tendency, their own faults to hide.
Sometimes never gracious enough to let others slide.
Wake up and be a friend to man.
Then your usefulness will constantly be in demand.

Give courage, faith, and praise to those you meet.
Your time will come when you need such a treat.
To brighten your day and help you along,
To fight this world's battle is no easy song.

Love one another is the Christian way,
Abide by this rule, and it will surely pay.
You'll have friends outnumbered in sincereness and best wishes.
These are foods that make up life's best dishes.

Foods that make you so strong, you can achieve any height,
Without well-wishers and people to cheer you constitutes a lonely plight.
So do unto others as you would have them do unto you.
Then your life will be beautiful, and you'll have God's blessing too.

Be Good to Yourself

You are growing in grace
You're seemingly winning the race
Yet, it's hard to maintain
All the profits that you gain.

People will fool you
Sometimes merely just use you
To gain for themselves fame, fortune, and glory
Oft times this is the sad, sad story.

Be wise, be good to yourself, look around you
Know when you're overworked and tired too
Good health is truly your very best friend
It'll stick by you through thick and thin.

When you become ill and no longer able to do
Big and little favors that you are used to
Friends, neighbors, and relatives oft cast you aside
That's the way of this world in which you abide.

So remember to yourself always be true
Good health and faith in God will see you through
It's nice to be kind and help your fellow man
But when you're sick, you are no longer in demand.

It's not being selfish when you say no
Your mind and body should tell you how far to go
Let it not be said people worked you to death
They'll sometimes do it until you draw your last breath.

Be Good to Yourself (Cont'd)

It's a shame to make such a terrible statement
But the world today readily has your replacement
Do what you can but always keep your good health
In comparison to money, it's the greatest wealth.

Riches and gold are hard to beat
But a clean healthy mind and body will always defeat
Obstacles, trials, and troubles that come your way
Good health will do what money can't pay.

Rich men at times would give all their wealth
In exchange for a life of constant good health
What does it profit to have money to spend
When you're physically unable to enjoy it in the end.

February 3, 1986

Count Your Blessings

How great it is to snuggle up at home.
When cold chilly icy weather almost freezes your bones.
Blessed with the comfort of a nice warm place to live,
Thankful and grateful that this God did give.

Means and ways to actually subsist,
With clothing, food, and shelter things many have missed.
So count your blessings each and every day.
It was God who made it possible for you to live this way.

February 9, 1988

A Recipe for Living

Work and no play is not good for the soul.
You reap poor benefits and achieve no goal.
"Rest is for the weary," is what they say.
Don't become weary. Play a little each day.

Make yourself smile to retain your beauty.
Mix with others that's your solemn duty.
Be kind to yourself is a very good slogan.
Good food and entertainment will keep you from boredom.

So let us live one day at a time.
Take exercise, rest in bed won't cost you a dime.
Be good to yourself whenever you can.
Maybe you'll live to be a very wise old man.

Make Each Day Count

Today is yesterday's tomorrow.
Time is something you cannot borrow.
Do your best from day to day.
That's the motto that makes things pay.

If by chance a task can't be completed, schedule it for another day.
Work left over must be finished, get it together is the best way.
If a task is once begun,
The old saying goes, never leave until it is done.

Faithful servants always abound in plenty.
The Bible states you'll be ruler over many.
Continue in this vein, and you'll always succeed.
Yesterday's recall you'll never need.

July 9, 1986

Hold Your Peace

If you can be quiet at the right time,
You can save many a heartache, maybe a crime.
Heartaches are sad, they make us frown.
They usually hurt and get us down.

If you can hold your peace and count to ten,
Things can be beautiful once again.
You won't have to ever take back things you've said,
That could hurt the living and maybe the dead.

Although you are hurt deep down within,
Hold your peace, and you will win.
Favor, love, unity, and self-respect,
For not making that scene, one you may always regret.

Always think twice before you speak.
It doesn't hurt to sometimes be humble and meek.
You may be right but may lose a best friend.
Now what did it profit you in the end.

True friendship is hard, not easy to come by.
Weigh every angle before you ever reply.
You may be angry as angry can be.
Forget your feelings, and you will see.

Hold Your Peace (Cont'd)

Life can be beautiful if given a chance.
It can equal to a song and a dance.
Tuck those old feelings somewhere far away.
Friendships will grow more meaningful each day.

As time goes by, *great love* will heal every wound.
Mistakes we've made will come to light soon.
So don't be too hasty in speaking again.
The one you hurt could be your very best friend.

Success

Success is for the eager who dare and do.
It is not for the idle who sit around and stew.
If success be your goal then do not brood.
Effort is what it takes, it is just like food.

You must have nourishment to survive.
So must success in order to thrive.
Push onward and upward every day.
Use your God-given talents in every way.

That's the challenge that all confront.
Keep the will, desire, and effort always in front.
Little do you know you may be close to your goals.
Just when things are darkest light usually unfolds.

Get Up and Get Busy

Bright daylight is pouring through your window glass.
Don't let all the entire wonderful day glide completely pass.
Get out of that bed and find something to do.
There's always a task just waiting for you.
Every day let your wisdom grow.
Think of tasks undone, let your usefulness show.
Choose each day a task to perform.
One that'll brighten your day, weathering out the storm,
At the end of the day, you'll feel great about yourself,
Because long-awaited tasks no longer were put on the shelf.

February 8, 1988

Be Aware of Accidents

Accidents can be serious even a minor fall.
They can put you in stress and behind the eight ball.
Your progress slows down, and you can't achieve,
The things you have planned and in which you believe.

A part of your life may have been hurt in the fall.
You're surprised to know some things can't be done at all.
Your ability to work, maybe simply to write,
Your poor hand could hurt as if been in a fight.

Well, it takes a strong will to stage a comeback.
Pick up loose ends and get things back on track.
But try you must, since life goes on.
Just keep up your courage until all work is done.

Leisure Time

Leisure time can be useful time too.
All time should be made to pay off for you.
Time wasted, one can never regain.
So don't let your leisure time go completely down the drain.

You can use your brain and also look at the soaps.
Plan something to do and do not mope.
Get something done that is pleasurable, maybe an art.
Two things can be done if you're very smart.

Knitting, drawing, painting, and writing are just a few tasks.
Many things can be accomplished as the day goes past.
Now don't let a day go by without something to show,
That the many hours spent didn't help you grow.

The Ways of Life

Life can be a bed of roses,
If you can only withstand all the knocks pains and bruises,
That oft come from your fellow man.

You got to be strong to live in this world,
Full of people hating to see you get ahead.

The only blessing they want for you is,
That you forever stay in the red.

You may go far as you journey on,
Accomplishing much in this struggle for life.

But fate has its many fights right back,
Filling your life full of chaos and strife.

Oh, God! Please put on this troublesome earth,
A bounty of peace, love, and goodwill.

Bless all of Your dear children, God,
So their uttermost dreams may be fulfilled.

Age, Only a Number

Who wants to grow old, neither I nor you,
However, birthdays come, so don't be blue.
Life can be happy as time goes by,
Sometimes it is too short, so don't sit around, brood, or cry.

Find something useful to do that's really worthwhile.
Don't let a day pass without a great big smile.
So be of good cheer as you pass along.
Let each day that comes be a melodious song.

As you go down the road of life each day,
Don't ever forget to get down on your knees and pray.
Thank God each day for His kindness and for allowing you to grow old.
He'll bless and endow you with greater wisdom, I'm told.

To grow wiser is not a gift just passed around.
Through age and experience, it is something found.
Be proud to have aged, and be grateful too.
For long life on this earth is only granted to a few.

Be a Well-wisher

Do unto others as you would have them do unto you.
That's what the Bible says, and I'm sure it is true.
If you desire God's blessings, you must follow the golden rule.
Speak no ill of anyone, and always keep your cool.

Love one another is a definite way to success.
Peace of mind will come your way with loads of happiness.
The truth will always be in your favor when spoken from day to day.
Then you can look everything and everyone in the face, come what may.

Help the downtrodden find their way back up.
Don't be a part of stepping on them, grinding them to a pulp.
They are only human like you and subject to err.
Your sympathy and understanding could make that mistake not reoccur.

Try not to be covetous or let jealousy or envy prevail.
Be a true well-wisher to friends, neighbors, and all whom success did hail.
Join the ranks of well-wishers, to all who come your way.
Be sincere and give them your blessings, success could happen to you any day.

Now take this advice, and spread it all around.
It doesn't behoove any of us to push anyone down.
Be your neighbor's keeper at home, school, church, work, and play.
This is what is needed in a chaotic world like today.

August 21, 1986

Be What You Are

If you want to be happy as you plan what to do,
Remember don't ever bite off more than you can chew.
Life's lonesome journey is hard at its best,
So down its rough path, you'll also need some rest.

Rest for the weary is what lots of us need.
But this good advice we seldom do heed.
We continue to push what we need to stop.
It wasn't meant for everyone to be on top.

Accept what you are.
Be thankful too.
That God has blessed you,
With health and a family that's true.
There is room in the world for all.

That Monster Prejudice

Prejudice should be a thing of the past.
Yet this demon seems to last and last.
Truly prejudice is a very ugly word.
The meaning of which should scarcely be heard.

The youth of today don't understand such.
Its older folks going about talking too much.
If they'd be quiet and let the youngsters be.
There'd be no difference between you and me.

Prejudice is a very nasty old thing.
It tears lives apart and always brings,
Unhappiness, sorrow, destitution, and dislike,
A world full of hatred and people going on strike.

It is God who made us, one and all.
Made in His image so none of us should fall.
He created us to do His solemn will.
Foster His teachings and His word fulfilled.

Equality is what it's all about.
With that old prejudice would no longer sprout.
So, parents, it's left to you to join the children of today.
Leave them alone, and they'll join hands and play.

With prejudice gone and out of our lives,
America will grow stronger; thus, the entire nation thrives.
A better place to live in peace and harmony,
A paradise on earth for the whole world to see.

February 8, 1988

The Lonely World of Today

Loneliness is like a disease; it eats into your very soul.

Being a victim, or observe others, the likes cannot be told.

If you're strong you can fight it, by finding something to do.

To sit and watch loved ones and others hurts and makes you blue.

There should be some way of changing this gruesome world outside.

Afraid to go to the corner, less some snipes take you for a ride.

You can't be friendly with your neighbors, as they stop you at the door.

You can't blame them in a way, because they don't know what's in store.

Now you try to see TV as a definite way out.

But when you hear and see the news, the deaths, shootings, and crime,

You wonder what it's all about.

So you must try to find something wholesome to do, and think of constantly day and night.

This is your life advice, you must man and guide it so it will always be happy and bright.

Wonders of Retirement

Retirement is an outstanding achievement and a worthwhile goal.
Today retirement doesn't mean you're growing old.
You've just reached a great peak, stage, and significant milestone in life.
There will be days filled with more contentment and less with strife.

You've won an uphill battle with the children "Dear."
They'll love, cherish, and respect you, do not fear.
They'll sing praise to you as to how you molded their lives day by day.
You've been a beautiful person and a wonderfully inspiring teacher as
you paved their way.

You've come to a brand-new beginning, we must all confess.
We wish you good health, peace, joy, and contentment showered
with loads of success.
You'll be missed by principal, teachers, staff, and parents too.
They are all aspiring for this accomplishment and eventually become
just like you.

Wide open doors are now available to you each and every day.
You can come and go in your own special way.
What fun it is to travel, it's the latest fade.
Such leisure time will make your husband especially glad.

Wonders of Retirement (Cont'd)

Time to rest and time to play.
Choose a good hobby, it will always pay.
You've come to the peak, place, and crossroads, but you must travel along.
Live one day at a time, and life will be a song.

Look toward the future with a great big smile.
You've conquered a glorious fete that is so worthwhile.
God bless you and now congratulations are being sent your way.
We're proud you reached RETIREMENT WHAT A WONDERFUL DAY.

June 1, 1989

A Poem

To have life on every hand,
One gets to the point it's hard to stand.
You gradually become so it's hard to think,
People not strong often turn to drink.

To have set your goals and standards high,
Withstand hardships and did not cry,
To have accomplished things that you have planned,
Then all at once changed by mortal man.

To be controlled and don't know why
You have to undergo such and that's no lie.
When you have tried and done your very best,
Then folks come along and won't allow you to rest.

Why does this world have to be so mean?
That it won't allow you to even seem,
To be what you really are and know,
Mad because God has let you grow.

Regardless of all evil, they've thrown your way,
You've had the ability to cope and stay.
Stable in mind and physically fit,
Stronger in determination, fit, and endowed with more grit.

You've more ability to ward off the troubles they cause,
Fight continually back and do not pause.
You labor on each day in your own efforts to succeed,
Paying less attention to them and their greed.

A Poem (Cont'd)

You never heed be the stumbling blocks they put in your path each day.
You walk over them, delete and continue to pray.
Thus, you become endowed with a stronger will to go on.
This you continue until the battle is won.

Push onward and upward till you conscientiously fulfill,
Your dreams and high hopes to rise to the top of the hill.

All folks in this world are not the same,
There are some still that and always will remain,
Fighters and pluggers, as long as life lasts,
Knocks and kicks they've learned to look past.

They know how to let those monsters become food to grow,
Enabling them to push forward even though it may be slow.
Oh, people and the world, may hold someone back,
Why not give them a second chance and use more tact?

They may give or leave some contribution to all,
If you weren't constantly trying to make them fall.
Now take this message from someone who's old,
You're keeping your country backward, I'm told.

When you oppress people with talents and gifts,
Coming from God, you are out of your wits.
If they are used they'll multiply and grow.
Now you must believe me folks because the Bible says so.

A Poem (Cont'd)

Let people alone regardless of color or creed.
Give them a chance to get out, live, and succeed.
Don't hold them back if they're more talented than you.
Their wisdom and knowledge may help see you through.

It has been known for years dated way back,
We can all learn from a child, and that's a fact.
So give each child an equal chance,
Don't hold them that let them advance.

This is America, don't try to enslave,
Children's aptitudes that may help you pave,
A way to a brighter tomorrow and thus a grander nation,
Gaining respect from all under creation.

The things in the past don't bring those old grudges back.
Accomplishments made please keep them intact.
Put yourself in the place of others you see.
They're human and want to live like or better than you and me.

The world is in turmoil and grows worse each and every day.
If you don't straighten things out, we're all going to pay,
With your minds closed to just holding folks back,
Other countries are invading and striking where you lack.

Children are your future leaders,
Invaders need no guns.
They're hurting America's finest and greatest sons.
Wise up, America, let Education prevail.
Keep it free for all, and do not fail.

A Poem (Cont'd)

All the children should have the same advantage,
Your narrow-mindedness is to your disadvantage.
If you lose your youth, you have nothing to gain.
Without leaders, the country will never be the same.

Give equal opportunities in housing and the job,
You've let folks down and actually did rob,
People of their birth rights born right here,
Because of their color, you did interfere.

Give them a chance to actually thrive,
Live above poverty and stay alive.
It's about time you began to awaken,
If you don't, we are all going to be shaken.

This country and maybe the entire world may be destroyed in time.
When you lose your youth and constantly ban.
Monsters living here on every hand.
Because you are not following God's plan which is so divine.

He put us all on this earth to be,
Brothers and sisters and neighborly.
Live together in peace and constant goodwill,
Keep each other up and not drag him downhill.

It can be done if you only but try,
To do right by all, you'll be blessed by and by.
A world with peace and harmony,
It is a world where everyone is constantly free.

A Poem (Cont'd)

Free to go and come wherever he chooses,
Knowing he will gain and never loses,
His actual life, dreams, and hopes along the way,
As he travels along in this ole world of today.

Now there'll be always something to look forward to.
Knowing your potential and just what you can do,
Knowing you have a place and a wonderful chance,
To live in America, let alone the world and advance.

Retirement Thoughts

If you rise up bright and early all the time,
And work and work never earning a dime.
You often wonder when a change will come,
Forever cooking, washing, and cleaning a house becomes pure boredom.

Work with pay, surely motivates.
No pay, so at times you just stay in bed late.
Finally, you began to realize what a fool you've been.
Get smart, get more rest, exercise, with good health you'll win.

Energy and foresight will come your way.
You'll think of things that'll brighten your day.
You'll gain a better disposition and a winning smile.
Retirement and old age will be more meaningful and awfully worthwhile.

February 9, 1988

The Importance of Relaxation

Relaxation is something we all need.
Money is fine, but many have too much greed.
What is it to be rich, sick, and ill at ease?
The rich man at times prefers good health than his hands to grease.

Good health stems from knowing how to relax.
Most people's lives are cut off and shortened by that axe.
Find out what you most enjoy.
Men, women, and children, whether a girl or boy.

Relaxation is like food for the brain,
Digest it at all times, and life won't be a strain.
Too much work and no actual play,
Makes Jack a dull boy, it will stand in his way.

What relaxes me may not relax you.
Find out the things that won't make you blue.
Engage in that activity or art.
Change is good to get you ready for a fresh start.

Animals

The Baby Chipmunk

I saw a baby chipmunk, as cute as he could be.
He stood on Sylvia's doorstep looking boldly at me.
He was so very, very tiny, only a few inches tall.
He was light tan all over, and you'd think he wanted to call.

He probably wanted to come in to look for his little playmate.
Maybe he got lost from his mother, oh, what a terrible fate.
He became very startled when Rea came walking near.
That tiny little chipmunk did certainly disappear.

He was so very frightened, he just vanished in thin air.
I'm sure he learned a lesson in his moment of despair.
Yet no one would do him the tiniest bit of harm.
Maybe take him to school so the kids could see his charm.

My Special Birdie

There is a little bird singing all around my house.
Now he lights upon my windowsill and gets quiet as a mouse.
Do you know what he's chirping about as he goes his merry way?
Maybe he sings that same little song, all the live long day.

Does he sing because he's happy, or does he sing because he's sad?
Could be he's trying to tell you something, let's hope it's not very bad.
He needs a friend just like you and me.
Maybe he's lonesome and doesn't want to flee.

He might just make a fine little pet.
But his home is on the outside, don't ever forget.
Water and breadcrumbs may be just the thing.
Place them within his reach, then he'll surely sing.

He'll come back daily for you to see.
Then he just might fly a bit closer to thee.
He'll learn to love you as time goes by.
He'll sing his heart out, and you'll be the reason why.

The Hungry Little Bird

Chirp, chirp, chirp went the little bird as he flew up in the tree.
He left his food and everything because he was afraid of me.
As he looked down on the ground to see what I was going to do,
He realized I wouldn't harm him, so back to the ground he flew.

He ate and gobbled up all he could see,
The grass seed and crumbs but always kept one eye on me.
Fluttering here and fluttering there,
He ate and ate without a care.

Then all at once, a great big dog from nowhere came rushing by.
Then that little bird away did quickly fly.
Frightened and nervous and shaken just a bit,
I too ran to the house also scared out of my wits.

February 1988

Anniversaries

Happy Anniversary

Anniversary Greetings

Thanks to God prevails today.
You have certainly come a very long way.
It was He who helped to see you through.
A marriage of bliss and happiness too.

Of course, there were trials, tribulations, and the rest.
But you survived and stood the test.
Many have helped and aspired to reach the goal from the start.
But obstacles came along pulling them apart.

Fifty years of marital life.
Loving and living together as man and wife,
You're to be congratulated by one and all.
You've climbed the ladder of success and standing tall.

Yes, you've been and are role models to your children, relatives, and friends.
They all love and respect you and will until the end.
May you be blessed to live and enjoy many more fruitful years.
As you keep faith in God whom you've always held so dear.

July 12, 1989

Aspirations

My Goal

To become a teacher in Washington, DC,
Was my dream as you clearly can see,
I stuck it out through thick and thin,
Until the time it just had to end.

To retire from a wonderful position like this,
Makes me proud and yet all of you I'll miss.
Parents administrators, principals, and pupils too,
You have all been great to see me through.

It gave me pleasure as I traveled around,
Telling all my friends the name of the town.
Where I taught school from day to day,
Of course, "The nation's capital," I would say.

I've watched the district schools grow each and every year,
Now our dear superintendent needs to have no fear.
The pupils now get that reading, writing, and arithmetic,
The *three* things needed to pass a test quick.

Teacher, it's hard, but you always come through,
You're shining stars to the children, isn't that true?
So give them all you've got, you'll see your reward,
As they successfully stepped out into the many fields of board.

Babies/Children

Little Baby Fair

Here's to a little lady fair
We all think of as very rare
Never, never a minute still
Always doing her little will
Playing, singing, dancing reading
Whatever it is she must be the leading
We watch her closely every day
Wishing her the best in every way
That she achieves her aims and goals
That will take many, many years to unfold.
We ask You, God, to guide her right
As she goes through life both day and night
Protect her for us, Father dear
For our love for her is so very sincere.
Help her to understand thy will
In daily tasks, she does fulfill
Bless her with courage that she sustains
Life's many troublesome aches and pains
Now last, oh, God, let her faith be true
In herself, mankind, and mainly in You.

Birthdays

An April Birthday

To have been born in April was your fate.
Yes, the —— of April that's the date.
It's been a happy day through the years.
Enjoying it with friends and family dear.

You've grown a little older, but wiser too.
You've learned how to live and see life through.
You know how to tackle problems along the way.
And make life harmonious from day to day.

Continue to be like a breath of spring
Flowering and budding as the birds sing.
Blessed with favor from God, yes, friends and man,
Showing assets that glow on every hand.

So may this birthday be a happy one.
And your many wishes come true, and His will be done.
May you be blessed by God in heaven above,
And showered with the gift of His constant love.

Happy birthday, Gladys!

A Birthday Message

Another birthday, oh, that's great.
Just to be alive and enjoying this date.
The day you were born is one to remember.
Whether it's in March, April, or November.

Birthdays come, and birthdays go.
But in many ways, we grow and grow.
Some get older and wiser too.
Yet, there are some who know not what to do.

Birthdays should be milestones in all our lives,
Progress should be seen as we continue to strive.
If you have accomplished just one little feat,
That makes living worthwhile and that can't be beat.

To be able to look over the many years,
And have a feeling of pride though it may bring back tears.
Things you remember in the days gone by.
Good things and sad things that helped the years fly.

So as your birthday comes up, each and every year,
If you put your best foot forward, you'll have no fear.
Regrets and failures will be only few,
And on each birthday, you'll be happy and very seldom blue.

A Special Birthday

You're such a wonderful person,
Deserving in many a way.
That's why God has given you the privilege to enjoy this special day.

When you've reached a ripe old age.
You've accomplished a very great feat.
Able to do your daily tasks and get around as you do can't be beat.

He's smiled on you especially because you are one of His chosen few.
You have proven yourself a Christian, in everything you do.

So on this day be thankful,
For your blessings far and wide.
Continue to lead a life that is clean and holy,
And He will always be at your side.

Christmas

Christmas Eve

It's Christmas Eve, can't you tell,
The air is filled with a glorious smell.
With goodies to eat and festivities
to attend,
Happiness and joy that hopefully won't end.

The Christmas tree takes on a special glow,
This is the night for its special show.
With candles and candy canes decked all about,
Giving color to its branches all stretched out.

The stockings are filled for all to see,
To make the children all just shout with glee.
Presents and toys are placed under the tree,
Put there to bring happiness, joy to the entire family.

Someone is knocking, oh, who could that be,
Carolers who've come to sing to you and me.
Sing about the Christ child born, sing of His birth,
He who was born Christmas day to bring peace,
And goodwill on this earth.

December 7, 1985

Santa at Christmas Time

Santa Claus is such a dear,
He always comes this time of year.
With his sack all filled with toys,
Made especially for good girls and boys.

Now I'm sure he has a treat,
For Mother and Father to make complete,
A wonderful job of spreading all around,
Happiness, peace, joy, and goodwill that know no bound.

December 7, 1985

Christmas

Christmas is a time to be merry and to be of good cheer.
It's a time to be thankful for your many blessings throughout the year.
Reach out and greet others as you pass along the way.
Spread love, goodwill, sunshine, and "Yuletide best wishes," now and every day.

Christmas Thoughts

A daughter and a son-in-law like you are hard to find.
So here's a little Christmas prayer for being so very kind.
May God bless the two of you.
May your many wonderful dreams come true.
This Christmas and the oncoming New Year.
And your whole life will be full of cheer.

Love, Mother

Christmas

Christmas is a time for love,
And giving thanks to the Father above,
Whose son was born on that glorious day,
That the entire world celebrates in a special way.

We send glad tidings to one and all,
Spreading happiness and joy beyond recall,
Brotherhood, friendship, and peace abound,
Triumphantly reigning from town to town.

Families gather from far and near,
Sharing gifts and blessings with those they hold dear.
It's a time for reverence and yuletide prayer.
Time to glorify God and seek guidance for the oncoming years that
are often bleak and bare.

Christmas time illuminates the hearts of men,
Gives them an unusual joy deep down within.
Peace abounds the likes of which can't be measured,
Christmas is the time of year that will always be treasured.

Faith

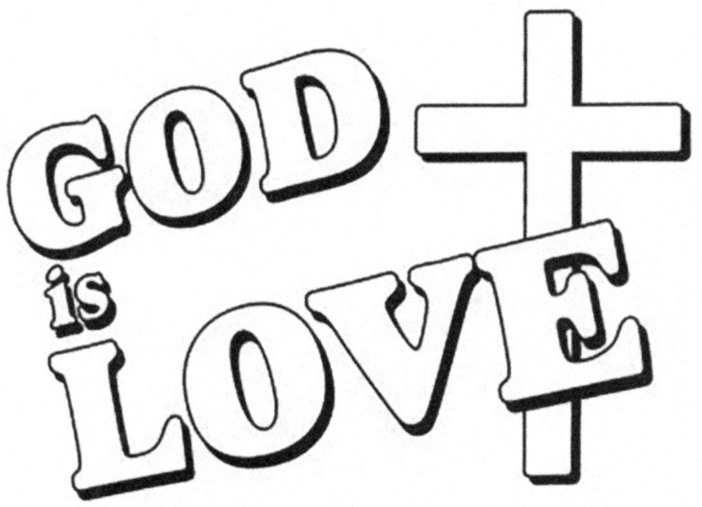

Traveling God's Way

There's a road out there that leads to the top.
When you get on that road, don't you ever stop.
There are many roads that you may choose from.
But only one road is the right way to come.

There are highways and byways that you will pass.
You'll continue to encounter them as long as life lasts.
Take time to decide where you wish to go.
Travel carefully and slowly so you can grow.

Select wisdom and knowledge, and your choice will be right.
Then the road you travel could make all your days bright.
Be careful of the road with crooked curves, shortcuts, and snares.
It may be the road to destruction so beware.

Take advice from your elders who won't steer you wrong.
To be sure you are right they could come along.
Learn to map out your plans before you start.
There are so many roads, and it's hard to tell them apart.

The shortcut may actually seem alright.
Remember, reaching the top is no easy plight.
Oft times the road is dark, lonesome, and drear.
It is all up to you so be careful dear.

You must travel the straight and narrow way.
That is the path from which you must never stray.
You'll wind up a success in any path you choose.
Because that is God's way, and you cannot lose.

God's Love

Always remember, God loves you.
He will always see you through.
Upheavals, storm clouds, woes and snares,
Always know that the Master cares.

He loves us all from day to day.
As we walk this lonesome narrow way.
He is with you as you toil along,
Don't fret children God makes us strong.

With Him, by your side, you'll always win,
Any race in life that you begin.
He's at the start of each daily task.
For His help, you need only ask.

Continue to keep on praying; He'll help you out.
He's your friend and mine without a doubt.
Surely something good will become of all this.
With God by your side, you can never miss.

God's Way

Time waits for no one, it is said,
So be up and ready to make your daily bread.
Put your best foot forward each and every day.
Then He'll make two steps to show you the way.

He helped you in time of need.
So you can do likewise, be a friend indeed!
Render some service to your fellow man.
Your reward will be great, cause that's God's plan.

Speak words of comfort and encouragement to those fallen along the way.
They need your prayers and love to guide them each day.
Now priceless are those who've stood the test.
Cause living God's way has proven the very best.

A Bright, Shining Soul

To be clean on the outside
And cleaner still on the inside,
Makes for a bright, shining soul.
That's something God expects from us
both young and old.

First, we must be kind to each other.
Trust your neighbor as a brother.
Always lend a helping hand,
To those in need and cannot stand.

Speak no words of evil or reproach.
But say kind words and help to coach,
A forlorn soul along life's way,
Who needs some help from day to day.

Cast not stones at anyone.
Your day of reaping may have just begun.
Clean your own house, let it be first.
There will be no time left for such an outburst.

A God-given Right

Freedom is a God-given right.
All races and creeds want to enjoy it if they are very bright.
If they are dumb, it's a right they're entitled to.
Freedom to speak, walk, talk, and reside are long overdue.

To live and be left entirely alone.
To do your will in your own little home.
Eat and be merry is not carrying things too far.
Freedom to pursue your dreams even if it's becoming a movie star.

The many races have a right to live their own lives.
They should be free from continued meddling eyes.
Freedom should be a priority each and every day.
Folks want happiness in their own special way.

America you're known as the land of the free.
Make this motto apply to any minority.
Let freedom bells ring and resound over valley, hill, and dale.
All races will live peacefully and happily forever, without any fail.

Faith to Live By

To awaken fresh bright and early each day
Is a blessing from God in His holy way.
To know the feeling deep down within,
That He is beside you, and you'll always win.

Though problems arise and confront you each day,
You'll find a solution, just constantly pray.
Rely on your faith, as the days go by.
He stood by you in the past, hold your head up high.

He's there don't forget, just get on your knees.
In Jesus's name just ask for your greatest needs.
He'll come to your rescue in His own time.
Just keep on believing, and everything will be just fine.

So smile and be happy. Though there's a deep hurt inside.
Be kinder to your enemies, and hold on to your pride.
Your strength will grow to meet the years ahead.
Hopefully accomplishing your dreams, aims, goals, and ambitions
instead.

August 6, 1987

God's Love

Through the sunshine and the rain,
He'll certainly come to see you again.
In Him, if you always believe,
Your uttermost dreams you'll surely achieve.

He's your Redeemer, Savior, and friend,
Who'll always stand by you until the end.
So on the Father in heaven above,
Continue to trust and give all your love.

He died on the cross so that all His children may live.
In this sinful world that He did forgive.
One and all as they traveled and went astray.
Showering His blessings as they returned to the straight and narrow way.

Stay Close to God

Stay close to God
For that's the only way
Stay close to God
He'll solve your problems today
He extends a hand
As our prayers demand
Stay close to God
Stay close, stay close to God.

Stand up for right
In everything you do
Stand up for right
And He will see you through
He will pave the way
Each and every day
Stand up for right
Stand up, stand up for right.

Give of your best
Just as you win your way
Give of your best
Why don't you try it today
God will do His part
Right from the very start
Give of your best
Your best, your best to God.

Stay Close to God (Cont'd)

Love one another
As you travel along
Love one another
And God will make you strong
He'll light up each day
As you pass this way
Love one another
Yes, love, love one another.

Join hands with God
So do it right away
Join hands with God
And you will never stray
He'll show you the way
It will surely pay
Join hands with God
Join hands, join hands with God.

There's a Road

There's a road that leads to the upward way.
We must all travel it as we live today.
We must be kind to each other as we go along.
Reach out and touch a brother, life's not a song.

Extend a helping hand, it will surely pay.
Give your best, that is God's way.
In the end, you'll be blessed for the good deed you've done.
Your inward glow will feel like warmth from the sun.

Let not a day pass without a good deed.
It'll come back to you double, that's God's creed.
In the end, you'll reap a reward that'll pay.
You'll be blessed by God and respected by friends each and every day.

You never know what tomorrow will bring.
We all hope our harvest will be a good thing.
Whatever the future might hold for you.
The seeds you've sown will surely come through.

May your harvest be good and not out of control.
That's determined by the life you unfolded.
So do unto others as you'd want for yourself.
Don't let your good deeds be put away on a shelf.

Life is too short to be marked in dismay.
Get on your knees, let God pave the way.
He'll surely bless you through constant prayer.
Ask Him to guide and keep you, His love is always there.

Achievement through Faith

To awaken fresh, bright, and early each day,
Is a blessing from God in His holy way.
To know the feeling deep down within,
That He is beside you, and you'll always win.

Though problems arise and confront you each day,
You'll find a solution, just constantly pray.
Rely on your faith as the days go by.
He stood by you in the past, hold your head up high.

He's there, don't forget, just keep on your knees.
In Jesus's name, just ask for your greatest needs.
He'll come to your rescue in His own time.
Just keep on believing everything will work out fine.

So smile and be happy, though there's a deep hurt inside.
Be kinder to your enemies, and hold on to your pride.
Your strength will grow to meet the years ahead,
Enabling you to accomplish your many wonderful goals, aims, and
ambitions successfully instead.

Fathers

A Tribute to Father

You're one in a million when it comes to dads
You've stood beside the children and kept them glad
You're always there at the right time
To keep them happy and make their life fine
You're a Christian at heart and taught them to be God-fearing
And loving and always ready to see
The good in all that they meet from day to day
Thus they are loved and blessed as they go on their way
Yes you're a father in a million, I am here to confess
May God always be with you and surely your days and years
He will always bless.

A Challenge to Fathers of Today

What would the world be without fathers?
They are just as essential and important as mothers.
They cannot be pushed in the background.
Today their role stands up way out so progress can be found.

So on this day let us give fathers honor and glory,
For life with a real father is a beautiful story.
The love, affection, and devotion a real father showers on his offspring,
Last and is remembered regardless of whatever life brings.

A real father should be a role model as he goes his way,
Setting good examples for his little ones day by day.
Then in his household, he'd be king.
The family will love him and his praises forever sing.

Hold your heads up, fathers now and to-be.
You are most essential in this world you see.
Your children, especially your son
Thinks you are perfect in this race you run.

You cannot stand just idly by,
And allow your little ones to be denied and cry.
Without clothing, food, and shelter
Their lives will become a complete disaster.

Plan for the children's future as you go along.
Teach them day and night, right from wrong.
Be strong in your discipline, yet never abuse
Of this, let them never accuse.

A Challenge to Fathers of Today (Cont'd)

Bring them up in the Christian way.
Teach them the love of God each and every day.
Worship and attend some church always bring them along.
Thus your children will learn to pray and be very strong.

Be a father of which your children will be very proud.
Educate them the best you can, they'll stand out in a crowd.
They'll be self-sustaining with futures bright,
Holding good jobs and having possibilities that are out of sight.

It's up to you, fathers, don't let the nation or anything hold you back.
You are the ones who keep the family in tack.
Stand your ground and fight for your rights.
You can win by just keeping your goal in sight.

Be happy today for there's a greater tomorrow.
Fathers will have a definite place in the days that follow.
Many of you already weathered the storm and passed the test.
May this day that is yours be your very best.

HAPPY FATHER'S DAY TO ONE AND ALL!

June 19, 1989

Finances

Finances

At times I lie in my bed awake,
Some days just before daybreak.
I think of things that lie ahead,
That should be done to keep me out of the red.

I muscle up some paper and pencil to,
Figure and figure to my fingers are blue.
How to make ends meet,
To keep me out of the red-hot seat.

My addition and subtraction are sometimes right,
But if I'm a bit sleepy, I don't seem so bright.
After careful scrutiny, it all comes clear,
My many debts I need not fear.

There is always a way if you can plan ahead,
Keep yourself out of the red.
It may be hard for you to do ounce by ounce,
But keep on it and the ball will bounce.

Friendship

He Passed This Way Once

One day at a time was his way of life,
Kind and gentle to others, not causing strife.
Doing his tasks and chores from day to day,
Gave him pleasure as he went on his way.

You know not the day, the minute nor the hour,
So give to each other a beautiful flower.
Let's smell the roses, while they bloom today,
We're not promised to see the next May.

It was God's plan to call him home,
He's made peace with his Maker never more to roam.
He found eternal rest, no pain or sorrow.
Life's worries and problems no longer will be a bother.

Now let us all do our very best,
To live for Jesus and will be blessed.
Assurance will be ours that God will find a way,
To brighten our paths from day to day.

Family and friends do not grieve,
Be kind to each other, only believe.
Into each life, some rain must fall,
Put Christ in your life, He'll save us all.

My Special Friend

You're all I need, you're all I desire,
Heaven must have sent you to light up my fire.
You're my guardian angel, my bright and shining star,
Your wonderful being can be felt from a far.
Where have you been in the many days gone by,
Now that we've met, time seems to just fly.
Yes, where have you been all the days of my life?
So many sad days that were filled with strife,
You've given me something to live for both day and night,
As thoughts of you make every single one bright.

Something to hope for, something to dream,
Knowing there's someone on which you can lean.
Peace for the soul and the weary mind,
Giving strength to push lonesome feelings behind.
You're much to be wanted and much to hold,
You know how to keep one from growing old.
Wit and humor with you does always abide,
Casting off shadows that rise with the tide.
Kind ways and words are always there,
You always have plenty of them to spare.
So take care of yourself, you're needed so.
You give me hope and that wonderful glow.

Friendship

To have a friend as nice as you,

Brightness my day through and through.

You make just living so worthwhile.

I can greet each day with a beautiful smile.

Peace I now know to no abound.

What joy you have given me by just being around.

Stay close, oh friend, let friendship grow.

It's welcomed by all the world, you know.

Together in friendship, all nations can stand,

Living in peace with God and their fellowman.

Friends

True friends are like diamonds, precious, and rare.
You just can't find them 'most anywhere.
So cherish the old ones who are tried and true.
They may seldom fool or leave you whatever you do.

Be faithful to your friends and give of yourself.
Dedication and loyalty must never be put on a shelf.
Praise and encouragement are needed by all.
Let them know you're with them in summer, winter, or fall.

A friend stands by you when you're up or down,
Comforts and supports you so you'll not fall to the ground.
So when you need a friend, if you've been tried and true.
Your friend will come running to hold and support you.

Friends are like diamonds, precious, and rare.
Let those you have always know you care.
You'll never be alone if you reach out and touch,
Those neighbors and friends who've loved you so much.

February 25, 1988

Funerals

Funerals

Peace and Joy and Eternal Rest

She gave her best.
Now she's gone to rest.
Cast all sorrow aside.
With the angels, she'll abide.

Heaven opened its gates.
There peace and joy awaits.
Now she's gone to that great tomorrow.
Where there's no pain or sorrow.

Be of good cheer,
Family, relatives, and friends dear.
You loved her, it's true,
But the Master loved her too.

Live with God each day.
Walk in His holy way.
So lift your heads up high.
You'll meet her by and by.

May 30, 1989

Graduations

Graduations

Graduation—a Milestone to Success

Congratulations are being sent your way,
Great steps forward always pay.
You've mastered and achieved a most essential goal,
Graduation is something to be proud of whether young or old.

Many have started and given up the fight,
Some fall by the wayside, leaving a future that's not so bright.
When you give your best the time goes fast,
You arrive at a success that will last and last.
Such an achievement can't be measured in money and land,
Education is something to be treasured and is forever in demand.

God bless you, (enter the name of your
choice), continue on your way,
You're a beautiful person who'll make it any day.

To a Sweet Graduate

Congratulations are being sent your way.
Great steps forward always pay.
You've mastered and achieved a most essential goal.
Graduation is something wished for, and one
is proud of whether young or old.

Many have started and given up the fight.
Some fall by the wayside in a future that's not so bright.
When you give your best, the time goes fast.
You arrive quickly at a success that will last and last.

Achievement of this nature can't be measured,
It's more valuable than money or land.
Education is something to be treasured and is forever a demand.
God bless you, (enter the name of your choice)
May success be yours as you continue on your way,
You are a beautiful little person who'll make it any day.

Halloween

A Halloween Goblin

Did you see that goblin with his eye on me?
He is just as funny as he can be.
Decked in his robe of black and white,
Hardly visible in the night.

I wonder who he is trying to scare.
Of course, he's unusual and a little bit rare.
He seems quite happy as he goes about,
Knocking on doors along the route.

Then he hands you a bag saying trick or treat.
All he wants is something sweet to eat.
It's Halloween, didn't you know?
Children all dressed up; it's a wonderful show.

Inspirational

My Conscience

I have a little something that goes around with me,
It is quite amusing I wonder what it could be,
Sometimes it's helpful and makes me very proud,
To have it close beside me, then I like to say out loud,
Thank you, little fellow, it was so nice of you,
To show me this and that and tell me exactly what to do.

At times it's a bit annoying when I can't always guess,
All the things it's saying, then I'm causing a little stress.
Sometimes I wonder what it is all about,
I wish someone would let me know, then I'd no longer pout.
Sometimes I just wonder if I am right or wrong,
Then my conscious decides for me, and I can sing a song.

Music, a Great Art

Music is a great art, one that reaches your soul.
It lifts most people up, whether they're young or old.
To listen to your favorite songs, when you're down and out,
Turns your day around toward a happy route.

There are all types of music in this world of ours. Classical, jazz, religious, hymns, spiritual, folk, country, rock and roll, and the like, you can listen to for hours, you can have your pick and enjoy one of your choice.
If you are at home and love to sing, you can add your voice.

Beautiful music can be heard on your radio or TV
Just find your favorite station, this does not have a fee.
Special occasions sometimes arise.
Concerts of all kinds often give you a surprise.

There are so many great artists of the past and today.
We're all very grateful that they paved the way,
To make you happy as life goes on,
Oft times bringing back memories that have faded and gone.

Memories that are joyful and sometimes sad,
Cherished thoughts of experiences that could have been good or bad.
What would life be like without music and song?
Both spread cheer and goodwill as life passes along.

March 10, 1988

To Me

As I sit at my window thinking of the past
I see many heartaches that last and last
I see many yesterdays faded and worn
I see struggles on struggle that I've constantly born

It's not very easy when you are baffled about
By man and the storms of life that turns you inside out
You must have courage and faith in God
So life will not always be a hill trod.

Happiness

Happiness is the wish of all who live on this earth.
It is sorted out by all, from the time of birth.
To be very carefree, happy, and gay,
Is something desired, each and every day.

So let us live one day at a time,
Enhancing it with joy divine.
Do something that brings out a bit of laughter,
To brighten your day and days thereafter.

Each day strive to put something in your daily plan,
That gives you a lift, regardless of what's at hand.
This is your life, you have but one.
Be happy if you can, it can be done.

Work and all play makes Jack a dull boy.
Take this little tip and do not destroy,
A chance to get out and have some wholesome fun.
A bit of recreation is good for anyone.

You'll not get weary along the way.
Rest and fun are things that always pay.
Life will be sweeter and longer too.
You'll be more useful if to yourself you're true.

Love One Another

Love one another as the saying goes,
be a friend to man don't be his foe.
Reach out and touch somebody's hand,
even though he may be from a foreign land.

Be a good neighbor and that's the way,
One pays heavenly debts from day to day.
Help the downtrodden regardless of race or creed,
He is a human who stands in great need.

Remember the aged they also need you,
With God's blessings, you may have become aged too.
They have paved the way all along,
So when you start out you will be strong.

Little children sometimes lose their way,
Be a big brother or sister to them and it will pay.
There are the homeless seemly the world's forgot,
Please don't leave them in the cold to rot.

Life without meaning is a sad, sad affair.
Please let all your brothers know you care.
When you have lived in this life and taken a stand,
The whole world will know that you're a man.

Sunday School Away from Church

A blanket of snow covers the ground,
The family is sleeping you can't hear a sound.
You sit on your bed and plan what to do,
To keep them all happy so no one feels blue.
The day must be filled with warmth and cheer,
To help bring sunshine to those you hold dear.

We'll sing songs of Christmas,
That will be great fun.
All can join in and bring in the sun.
We'll tell riddles and stories about Christmas time.
We can even listen to nursery rhymes.
We can eat all the goodies that we can hold.
Surely ice cream and cake although it is very cold.

We'll play with the games though many parts are missing,
If they can be found it will surely be a blessing.
Of course, there will be TV, we can't leave it out.
All the grown-ups here would surely pout.
Night draws nigh, and the day starts to end.
We're happy with what we've done, forgetting what might have been.

Please Forgive Me

Thank You, Thank You.
I truly must say God's here to help me in every way.
I'm just a tiny little dummy sometimes,
Can you forgive me? I don't always rhyme.

Many sad moments you have shared with me.
I have often been as mean as can be.
Forgive me God for saying many ugly words.
I'll try to do better than sometimes you've heard.

Of course, my sanity is often at stake,
To speak my mind gives that tension a much-needed break.
So please be patient I mean no harm,
I'm only human and can sometimes do wrong.

Life Applications

So You Made It to the Top

You've made it to the top, but what did you gain,
When selfishness prevails in your very domain.
You reign with harsh words, words of contempt,
Words that speak evil, you're no longer exempt.

You've grown older and much wiser too.
What a shame that wisdom doesn't see you through.

You know the Bible as the saying goes,
What does it profit a man to gain the world and lose his own soul.

Be kind to all though you're at the top,
You do not know just when there'll be a big drop.
The friends you pass on the way up,
You'll meet again when you've run out of luck.

So never allow success to go to your head.
That's a sign of not being very well-bred.
Always remember the people you knew,
Before your success grew and grew.

What goes up usually come down.
You'll meet those old friends so keep your feet on the ground.

They'll love you and continue to wish you well.
And tell the rest out there that you're still swell.

An Early Start

What a beautiful feeling to breathe the morning air.
There's peace and quietness and solace everywhere.
Your mind becomes clearer and easy to reflect,
On the many things in life, you must not neglect.

It's easy to plan for the coming day.
On days and months ahead, and events to come your way.
It's very wise to keep in sight,
Past and present happenings they may help guide you right.

Start your day with a cheery smile.
Put into it something that is really worthwhile.
The early bird catches the worm, it is said.
So venture out and don't be afraid.

Greet neighbors, friends, and passersby,
Your glow may be catching, now isn't that wise?
People you meet as you wind your way,
May help to cheer you and brighten your day,

Do a good deed today and tomorrow,
Time is something you cannot borrow.
If you by chance see a soul in stress,
Why not help him, then you God will bless.

An early start is what most of us need.
To get out the cobwebs and plant the right seeds.
Sow seeds of kindness and seeds that lead to success. Then, you'll reap and gather a harvest that outshines all the rest.

Directions to a Good Life

Love thy neighbor as thyself.
This will endow you with abundant wealth.
Do unto others as you would have them do unto you.
Your blessings will multiply if you do.

Speak no words of evil about any man.
Clean out your own house first; that's God's plan.
Cast no stones or rocks; they usually hurt.
You may not live in a glasshouse, but why dig up dirt.

Be kind to your fellow man; we all need help, now and then.
One doesn't know when his turn will come; to need a good friend.
Lend a helping hand when and wherever you can.
Let that be a motto for each and every man.

Don't blame others for the state you're in.
Look at your faults and try hard them to mend.
Stay away from folks that are evil and mean no good.
They'd poison you and your mind, if they could.

Mingle with those you know stand for right.
A life of crime is possible, one must be bright.
They are out there to get you, to pave their way.
Hookers, hustlers, and gangsters prey on innocent persons every day.

Stand up for the right, although sometimes you may be alone.
Right works out in the end, as time has always shown.
Last but not least, be good to your own self; then you will be strong.
You'll have the will and courage to withstand and fight any constant
wrong.

Housebound

When snow storms come and last and last,
Taking over the city with a great big blast,
Suddenly you're wondering what to do.
Is there food enough for all of you?

Should I go out in all this dreadful storm,
Icy and slick all the roads seem to have become?
No, no, no, I'll just remain inside.
Safe and snug from the weather outside.

Put off going out for another day.
Surely that is the very best way.
The flakes come down in a steady downpour,
It's set in for the night of that you may be sure.

What to do until the storm should pass.
Is your next thought as you peeped through the window glass.
On your front, you see people in distress,
Wondering how to clean away the snow's big mess.

All at once, you make up your mind.
Being housebound is going to prove just fine.
I'll find things to do that I've constantly put off,
Such as cleaning and decorating my humble abode,
Rearranging things to fit today's mode.

Housebound (Cont'd)

Living today is a constant thing.
One should find time to help home bring,
Beauty and charm as the days go by,
So take advantage of the storm and time will fly.

You'll be proud of the things you do.
They'll give you a lift through and through.
Make housebound useful I'm sure all of you can.
The more beautiful the home is an enjoyment to every woman and
man.

January 28, 1988

Home

Humble or luxurious, home is the place,
To live and enjoy a day of rest and grace.
Though not so attractive and given to finery,
There's no place like it or where one would rather be.

Home is what you make it, and up to those who there dwell.
It can be a heaven on earth or a pure living hell.
It can be just so beautiful inside and out.
A house is not a home where the inhabitants always fuss and pout.

Home is a place to come to when all else fails.
Those who live within its bounds should know how to smooth out the sails.
Their warmth, love, companionship, and understanding should always be aglow,
Giving one's worn-out spirit a chance to once more grow.

So in the very near future, try to touch base with a real home.
Let love, peace, and joy abide, then you'll never, never roam.
Your life will be different, your walk and talk not be the same.
Your home will be a bit of heaven on earth, as you play life's wonderful game.

December 30, 1986

The Art of Dance

What fun it is to dance and sing,
To banish your cares and have a fling,
And float through the air and just glide away,
To the melody of a song and just sway and sway.

To dance a light fantastic toe,
And step to the music will help to show,
You're alive, full of energy, and can enjoy that beautiful art,
Dancing to rhythm is something that comes from the heart.

The waltz is for the dreamer, most men and women can't do,
It's only been perfected by just a very few.
Today it's almost a thing of the past,
Many sit it out, its steps are not fast.

Dance is a way to give vent to your feelings.
It lifts you up as you get lost in the reeling.
You forget sad things, and that's very true.
Dancing to the music fades out the blue.

Dance is an art that can be performed at any early age. Little children now are going on stage.
It's wholesome recreation and a great profession too,
Knowledge of rhythmic steps can open new realms for you.

Rhythm comes from the soul; many are born with it.
Dancing to the sound of music is something they'll never quit.
If you are so fortunate as to be endowed with that rhythmic gift,
Don't let it waste, or you'll grow old and too stiff.

The Art of Dance (Cont'd)

Dance is for the old as well as the young.
Get out and enjoy it, life has just begun.
Keep step to the music, and you'll never grow old.
This wise old statement has been made through the years; I'm told.

Visiting Your Birthplace

Do you remember the place of your birth?
To me, it is one of the grandest places on earth.
What a wonderful place to come home to,
Visit friends, classmates, relatives, and folks you once knew.

Walk and drive around in places where one time you'd play.
See the growth of the city and the many changes taking place today.
What beautiful memories it brings to mind.
Episodes, encounters, and happenings you'd left behind.

Yet you become saddened when you are told one day,
That a friend or childhood playmate has just passed away.
All at once, you have a feeling of great remorse,
But as you retrospect you realize, life must take its course.

You sit down and think of the years that have passed.
Thinking how you've been blessed although trials continue to last.
You finally realize and give thanks too,
That God has spared you to see it all through.

As you count your blessings that come from above,
You become closer to God and filled with love,
Filled with courage and plans to live a better life each day,
Be a better friend to man, as you journey on your way.

November 6, 1986
Newport News, Virginia

Time to Reflect

To be alone is not always bad.
A chance to think and meditate oft makes one glad.
We all need time to plan our daily lives.
Time to reflect and envision a dream that may arrive.

To sit alone and think way back,
Of good times or bad times might take up a little slack.
Maybe give you a brighter perspective of the days to come.
Planning a better future may help some.

One is not always lonesome if he has something to do,
Some places to go, and people to talk to.
Life is what one makes of his time from day to day.
Give heed to your physical and mental health and find time for play.

Remember to be alone is not the worst thing in life.
You can make your own decisions with less strife.
Enjoy the peace and quietness of the day.
Ward off some oncoming stress that may come your way.

To be alone at times is important to all.
One must work out problems whether large or small.
To give your best in all your way of living,
Leads to success and a life with fewer misgivings.

October 20, 1986

Home, a Beautiful Place

If home is quiet and restful too,
And you have many things to do,
It's a beautiful place to be,
To relax and think is good for you and me.

You can make your plans from day to day,
And see them materialize in your own special way.
You can put into action your many thoughts,
And accomplish some of the things you've been taught.

Home should not be just a place to come to.
It should be where the heart lies and dreams come true.
People are different, and their desires are not the same.
First, know what you want, then others you won't blame.

Things that relax me may not relax you.
Understand yourself and to yourself be true.
Concentrate on things that give you a lift.
Know when to stop, go, and shift.

Place in your home things to enjoy.
Such as peace, love, and kindness, they never destroy.
Set a time to just simply rest.
Then you can always be at your very best.

The people in your home must always be on their toes.
A house is not a home as the saying goes.
It is up to you to make your house grow.
And become the home that you wanted so.

August 6, 1985

A Charming Home

To have a home where you can be,
The person you have dreamed of yearly.
To live each day as you so desire,
And sit at ease by your candlelight and fire.

To relax and do anything that comes to mind,
Surely you can always be nice and kind.
To man or beast or anything,
That comes your way as time might bring.

To have a home where peace abides,
Is something special in which to take pride.
To live in harmony from day to day,
Is most surely the God-given chosen way.

To love each other and give respect,
To all around you and constantly reject,
Unchristlike acts, and point of views,
That cloud your mind and your thoughts confuse.

To have a home where Christ comes first,
Things will never be at their very worst.
At all times safe, day and night,
Carefree always, no burdens in sight.

Peace will be there, joy and love.
Your prayers will be answered by God above.
You'll be that person you've always dreamed of.
He'll make it possible yes that man above.

A Young Girl's Dream

A beautiful home is a woman's dream.
From the time of birth her little eyes would beam,
As she played with her doll house with its flair,
Of toy furniture and dolls from everywhere.

As she grew older, her collection increased.
More expensive in taste not to say the least.
The houses became larger and the dolls did too.
They became more real as time just flew.

The dolls could wet, cry, and walk.
Some of them could actually talk.
But as the years went quickly by,
Her approaching womanhood made time just fly.

A big girl now and ready to design,
That beautiful home she's kept in mind.
From early childhood as she would play,
Hoping and hoping it would become a realization one day.
Along comes her knight in shining armor,
Sweeping her off her feet with a lot of glamour.
Wedding bells tolled from all over the place.
She's all decked out in beautiful white lace.

Next, her heart says to make life complete.
Is to realize that dream house and hear the pitter-patter of little feet.
Yes, these things make up a young girl's dream,
Captivating the one to formulate a beautiful team.

Inspired by my daughter, Silvia Daniels, 1988

Make the Most of Each Day

Today is the tomorrow from yesterday.
Did you put off something and let it get away?
Can you call back dear old father time?
He's a shrewd old fellow so just you mind.

Strive to put the best in all that you do.
Opportunities come, don't let them pass by you.
Make the most of each day as they come and go.
Then you'll be ready for any show.

Climb to the top, that should be your aim.
Keep on trudging then you'll acclaim great fame.
Be consistent in your efforts day and night.
Then surely my friend all will turn out right.

Don't get discouraged when sometimes you fail.
Success is just around the corner for you to nail.
Failure is just success turned inside out.
Continue to push, you'll make it without a doubt.

So let no todays be a tomorrow.
Time is something that you can't borrow.
Just forge ahead with all your might.
Make each today further accomplish your plight.

With this constant effort, you've got to succeed.
Fulfilling your dreams, and your every need.
Then you'll be a star in your own right.
You'll guide others to success with your shining light.

Saturday, January 5, 1985

Night Shadows

Darkness makes shadows on the wall.
They move about and seem so tall.
You'd think they were real and very much alive,
As they play in patterns that do a dive.

Hopscotch is the game the shadows seem to play,
Moving about in such a peculiar way.
Up and down traveling around the room,
Forming shapes of all sizes in the deepening gloom.

As light and darkness seem to meet,
The day has faded and about to greet,
Night time which is now well on its way,
And the dark shadows disappear and no longer play.

February 8, 1988

A Day at the Races

A day at the races is so much fun.
You haven't seen anything until you've seen the horses run.
Galloping and galloping down the way,
Each horse sets out to win that day.

The crowd lets out a very loud cry,
As the horses seem to literally fly.
Come on, come on, you can be heard all around,
People cheer their favorite horse as he bounds and bounds.

Puffing and leaping and running so fast,
Each jockey striving for his horse not to be last.
Surely you're hoping that your horse will win.
Even if he just places, you can watch people grin.

The Passerby

A passerby, I know not who,
Lifted my spirits through and through.
It helped me to start a brand-new day,
Gave me the strength to continue on my way.

If only others could be so kind,
This would make just living quite divine.
To be able to get off to an extra good start,
Puts you ahead of the crowd and lifts your heart.

Now you're feeling good and have peace of mind.
Hope for the days and plans to do tasks left behind.
Your thoughts have changed, you're no longer sad.
Your beautiful smile lets all know you're glad.

A friendly chat with someone passing by.
May help your day and cause time to fly.
Yes, just someone like this could become a friend.
One never knows what may happen in the end.

August 20, 1987

This Big Wide Beautiful World

The world about is big and wide,
All kinds of creatures live inside.
There are people, plants, and animals too.
All living and breathing finding things to do.

There is land and water and the sky so blue.
All made so beautiful for me and you.
People and animals inhabit this earth.
Trees, in the woods and forests, were here at its birth.

Fish in the waters and birds in the air,
Are a part of earth's beauty so unusually rare.
Hills and huge mountains rise up high.
Valleys and plains stretch out under the sky.

Horses, sheep, and cows now graze on this vast land,
Making living on earth so much easier for mortal man.
The land is spaciously inhabited by people of all kinds,
Who live in different countries formed by mankind.

Nations have sprung up all over the world.
Each having their own way of life and cultures they preserve and herald.
Cities and towns can clearly be seen,
Made up of roads, streets, houses, lakes, and streams.

Boats, trains, and airplanes carry man from place to place.
Man now has invented objects that go way up into space.
The world is so different from the time of its birth.
It's a beautiful and wonderful pleasure to live here on this earth.

February 8, 1988

Keep a Good Image

When you look at yourself in a mirror, what do you see?
There's the image that will follow you wherever you may be.
To others it has value, but to you, it may have none.
It tells a life about you when it's all said and done.

You can dress it up and paint it.
For any occasion that will fit.
However, just be sure it's not a fake,
Since it's your reputation that is at stake.

Outside oft inside as images go,
They reflect good or bad feelings that grow and grow.
Your inward self is the real you.
Why not let the good side come shining through?

A growing continence is a wonderful thing.
Its sparks come from that inward ring.
A frown depicts that sad sometimes ugly thought,
That people and your mirror actually caught.

A mirrored image is a reflection.
You are the one with the recollection,
Of the inside and the outside you,
So ever be mindful, to yourself be true.

A smile will usually never hurt you, so,
Just make your image grow and grow.
Even though a smile is off times just the cover,
Those wrinkles will lessen you'll soon discover.

Keep a Good Image (Cont'd)

Images are like shadows constantly following you around.
Good or bad, they are used by people all over town.
So let your image stand out way out.
With a pleasing personality, you'll stand tall without a doubt.

February 15, 1985

Blacks, an Ongoing Race

Black is beautiful and a color of which to be proud.
Stand up, Black folks, and shout it out loud.
It's a grand and wonderful color that won't fade away,
And becomes more enhancing from day to day.

Sure, Black is a beautiful race, as many people have said.
The race is like the rainbow, very colorful instead.
Its beauty is like the sunset way up in the sky.
Yes, a race of many colors. Don't ask why.

Now when it comes to the race's place in this very great land,
Blacks have earned one outright, they've had to fight and demand.
Up from slavery is the road they've had to trod.
It hasn't been easy, as they did onward plod.

Segregation and discrimination were and are monsters they've met.
They've dealt with them regularly, on that you can bet.
Many battles they've lost and many they've won.
Yet Blacks must hold to the future because the struggle is not done.

The world's many evils must be held in tack.
Blacks must find ways to combat these evils, less they hold them back.
You're a race to be admired and respected by all.
You've done almost the impossible and continue to stand tall.

Now Blacks have been pushed and shoved around on every hand.
Given less jobs and few opportunities, how could they stand?
Yet the race has survived through thick and thin,
Attaining many goals that many thought they'd never win.

Blacks, an Ongoing Race (Cont'd)

All things are possible if you only believe.
Blacks can make it to the top and constantly achieve.
Have faith in yourself, God, man, and your race.
Letting love for one another always takes place.

February 8, 1988

Learn to Relax

Rest for the weary is good for the soul.
We all need it to reach our goal.
Time to relax and time to play.
Should be part of your schedule every day.

Television is good, it takes your mind off things.
Music is fine, you might play and sing.
Read a good book, it's a definite winner.
Puzzles and games are not only for the beginner.

So remember there are things to help you along.
Use them and others to help you grow strong.
You will find that life will be awfully nice.
Just give thought to what you do more than once or twice.

October 12, 1986

Mothers

A Dedication to My Mother

To have a mother just like you,
Is more or less a dream come true.
For who could ask for anything more,
Someone who's loving and kind and you can adore.

You were all I could want for and admire.
From the cradle up you did always inspire,
The best that I possibly had to give,
To you and the world as I did live.

Mother all that I am I owe to you.
It was always you who saw me through.
You were there when I needed you most of all.
You were there to sustain me if I should fall.

May God bless your soul mother as you rest in your grave,
Away from hurt, harm, and danger, you God did save.
Oh death, thou didn't have any sting,
For heaven you know is a beautiful thing.

Dedicated to my mother, Mrs. Mary Wilson Carr
May 11, 1984

Daughters Are Mothers

A daughter is nice to have
especially when she becomes a mother.
You not only have her to love,
she gives you another,
To love and cherish daily,
making life more worthwhile,
Bringing back old memories
of when you were a child.

She is a mother now,
that helps her best understand right.
Her wisdom, strength, and knowledge
usually grow overnight.
Guidance and affection,
she must learn when to use,
Neither of these great attributes
should she ever abuse.

May 11, 1984
Dedicated to my daughters, Loreathea Fields and Silvia Daniels

Grandmothers

Grandmothers are special people,
To every girl and boy.
They are forever spreading love around
To give the children joy.
When children want a story
To grandmother they will go.
Cookies, candy, and goodies
On them, she will always bestow.

Love and kisses unbounding she will freely give,
To cheer her sad loved ones and help them live.
Her efforts are never tiring,
As she lends a helping hand,
Mending their cuts and bruises that they cannot withstand.

Endowing them with much-needed courage
As they face the oncoming day.
Planting seeds of kindness
In every loving way.

Grandmothers are jewels
That are sent from heaven above.
Planted here on this lonely earth,
To give little children love.

Mother's Day Blessings Sister

You're the best sister anyone could ask for,
and a wonderful mother too,
You always solve our problems,
and know just what to do.
So I send this little message,
to you on Mother's Day.
To let you know I'm grateful,
for all the kindness shown my way.

Whenever advice is needed,
you were always there for me.
You aided, guided, protected,
and loved me constantly.
May God bless you with happiness.
and constant peace of mind.
May your days be fruitful and many.
and filled with love divine.

The Love of Children

Mother, we love you very much and just want you to know,
As you go about your daily tasks, our love just seems to grow.
How strong is the bond and devotion we feel for you, dear,
It becomes even greater and deeper as we live from year to year.

You are such a wonderful mother and have proven it in every way.
Never, never doubting as you go along, come what may.
Constantly working, seeming never tiring,
As you reach out to help others and always continuously smiling.

You've made an image that stands above all,
Forever there at your children's beck and call.
We are proud of you, knowingly we can never repay,
Or send enough love and gratitude your way.

Blessings for you mother will surely come from above.
You've showered your children with everlasting love.
Thanks for many kind deeds you've done and still do.
And the many prayers and guidance to help see us through.

The Name Mother

To give birth to a child doesn't make you a mother.
As you go through life you will soon discover,
The word *mother* means taking care of your child,
Not just any old way, but in your very best style.

That style includes raiment, food, and shelter decked, and clothed in love.
Making a child blossom and grow, like flowers from showers above.
With this to grow on from day today.
How could too many children go astray?

Take time out for your offspring, and you'll never regret.
When they mature you'll be their special pet.
So when Mother's Day comes around, you'll truly fit.
The name and word *mother* in all its meaning and connotation,
Thus becoming a great hit.

Mother, a Role Model

Mother's Day is a day that should be observed all year.
Because mother is the foundation of this world that lives in fear.
It is up to mothers to guide the many youths of today.
And make this earth a haven and a better place for her little ones to play.

She must set examples for them, as she plays her role.
She becomes their model as they go about setting their goals.
It is up to you, Mother, to help establish right.
Crime is an ugly monster; you should be a leader in the fight.

Mother, you may not have a helper, millions and thousands do not.
But you must bond together and be strong, give life your best shot.
It's your family you're protecting. Motivating and giving a chance,
To succeed and find a place in the world that you can say you helped
to enhance.

May 1, 1987

To Mother on Her Day

Mother's Day is a day for celebration
the whole world wants to cheer.
Especially all the children
who love and hold you dear.
To them, your day means everything
from the moment the glorious sun rises.
May your joys be very, very many
and filled with beautiful surprises.

You're wished a day full of happiness
here's hoping the years ahead are bright.
May you be blessed by the Father above.
Being a mother you deserve that right.
This is your day so enjoy it
it was set aside just for you.
We love and honor you, Mother.
May God bless you all the years through.

May 11, 1984

A Tribute to Mother

She's just gone to rest so please don't fret.
God loved her too, on that, you can bet.
Dry your eyes do not weep.
Mother dear has just gone to sleep.
God called her home to His kingdom on high.
One day you'll meet her in the great by and by.
Now family and loved ones do not mourn.
Her life was beautiful from the time she was born.
Give thanks and praise because she paved the way.
For you to follow and live by, from day to day.

April 10, 1967

A Mother's Day Wish

You're a mother and a daughter who would make anyone very proud.
You always glow and stand way out in 'most any kind of crowd.
You are very, very thoughtful in most things that you say and do.
You let the very best in you, at all times come shine right through.

Your kind deeds are always visible to those you constantly meet.
Your winning smile and cheery manner are extended to all you greet.
I love you now and always and never want to see you looking sad.
That's because I'm pleased and happy when you are very glad.

Happy Mother's Day!

Life without a Mother

What is life without a mother, many of you can tell.
Was it hard growing up and life didn't treat you swell?
Well, there's a way to change; things should not remain the same.
Don't go about being angry, there may not be anyone to blame.

Life plays tricks on all of us, it's not for us to judge another's race.
If you don't understand the reason some things have taken place,
Just make the most of whatever you have, find friends with whom
to share,
Your uttermost emotions, dreams, and secrets, they sometimes have
sympathies to spare.

Of course, you miss having a mother, but be thankful she was there,
To bring you into this world, it was very much pain she had to bear.
So love her wherever she is on this special Mother's Day.
Make the most of your life and don't forget to continue to thank God
and pray.

A Tribute to Mothers and Womanhood

You're oft mother and father in many a home.
You've arrived at success though working alone.
You are to be admired by all to see,
The accomplishments you've made toward the future to be.

Don't ever let anyone create a doubt.
Your place in this world we couldn't live without.
So girls watch yourselves, you are the women to be.
Keep your heads up high, demand respect, and you'll see,

A beautiful life and future unfold.
Giving motivation to attain that most desired goal.
You can do anything if you stick to the many tasks begun.
Good jobs and opportunities will always come and be fun.

Women you are a gift to this cold cruel world.
You were made to be cherished, you are a real pearl.
You are a lighthouse for all who have lost their way.
You are shepherds for those who have gone astray.

Your untiring efforts in this world of ours.
Stand out in front through the many hours.
You take your stand whenever there's a need.
You push onward and upward and pay failure no heed.

May 22, 1984

A Real Mother Loves You

Be kind to your mother, love her today and tomorrow.
Then when she passes away to the great beyond, your head won't be bent in too much sorrow.
Give your best, honor and respect to her you owe.
She's your pillow of life, so do all you can to keep her alive so you can grow.

Mother will aid you to become more plentiful in work, wisdom, and health.
She's a store full of knowledge and will and can give you advice that leads to wealth.
She's gone through the paths you are treading just now,
Give her a break, listen, and she'll show you how.

You can step out in life and meet the challenges of today.
Along with God's help, she'll show you the way.
Now don't cast Mother away as an old has been.
She may be aged, but old trees can always bend.

She'll bend over backward to see you through.
To help you attain goals that you thought were impossible to do.
Now when you greet her any day and special days, give her a great big hug and kiss.
That will mean more to her because she'll know love made you do this.

Nature

Sundown

The sun is setting in the west.
We just don't know how God has blessed.
Each and every one of us, in our journey and travels from day to day,
As we walk along in His chosen way.

We all have much to be thankful for,
The wind, clouds, and rain at our door.
Such beauty is always there to behold,
The blue sky above with its heavenly light,
And the many stars that shine so bright.

There is the ocean and the sea with their glimmering glow,
Waves and tides dashing to and fro.
Sure we're enhanced by the soft white sand and fine green moss,
And the many seashells that the waves just toss.

There are short trees and tall trees all around,
Scattered all over country and town.
Their pretty green foliage gives such wonderful shade.
As their limbs spread out like an outstretched hand,
Inviting you there to sit or stand.

The world is such a beautiful place to see,
And just to think God made it for you and me.
I'm sure you are thankful and grateful too,
That God put you here on this beautiful earth,
To breathe this fine air and fragrance from early birth.

August 6, 1985

The Woods

The woods are full of noisy things.
Some crawl, some hop, some sing.
You'd be surprised at the sounds, joys, and fears,
These creatures can bring to your listening ears.

To live close to the woods each day,
Is a constant joy, I must truthfully say.
You can see, hear, and smell Mother Nature.
She's at her best as in the woods you venture.

As the four seasons come and gradually go,
Mother Nature always puts on a big show.
In the fall, the trees are a beautiful sight.
Standing tall in the sun and bright moonlight.

Winter is the most picturesque of all,
Dressed in blankets of snow the trees seem so tall.
They bow their heads to and fro,
Speaking to the passersby as they go.

Spring is the time you must enjoy.
That feeling is shared by every girl and boy.
Its green enchantment on trees and grass,
Always make you wish spring would never pass.

Finally, summertime is here.
Trees and flowers blossom everywhere.
Surely the woods have grown on me.
Flashing an image that I constantly see.

The Woods (Cont'd)

Now fall appears with its magnificent show.
Bright red, yellow, purple, and brown other hues that glow.
Surely the woods now have fashioned a most memorable scene.
Such magic colors and beauty many have never seen.

It's wonderful to live with the woods nearby,
The seasons come and go making the time just fly.
Life becomes more enjoyable from day to day,
As you watch Mother Nature's wonders stage their play.

October 5, 1983

Sailing the Waters

Dedicated to waters around Newport News, Virginia

—Have you ever been sailing on the waters blue?
Have you? Have you?
What did you feel as you glided along?
Did your quickening heartbeat sing a song?

A song of peace and blessed content.
Was it engulfed in your soul as you went?
As you journeyed further out to sea,
Land and water met, seemingly.

When the anchor was cast and the boat stood still,
Did the oncoming waves give you a thrill?
Tossing and swaying the boat all about,
Along came one that almost threw you out.

As you started back on the journey to land,
Did you remember to thank God for such a beautiful plan?
The serenity of such is only understood by a few,
Of earth, sky, and water too.

March 12, 1983

A Beautiful Day

A beautiful day just gets into one's very soul.
It gives you a feeling that you can attain 'most any goal.
When you look out at the morning light,
You glow as you see the sun so bright.

Oh, if only you could cry out aloud,
How great you feel and just how proud,
That you are here on this wonderful earth alive,
To smell the fresh air and continue life's drive.

Surely you too have felt this way.
Wouldn't it be great if such a feeling would stay?
Then you could always be at your very best,
Face the future and put old ills and perils at rest.

Nevertheless, life must have its rounds.
One must always be ready when change sounds.
Its time may be on a different beat.
You must be prepared to always stay on your feet.

A beautiful day can be appreciated by all.
Weather-wise it's great, but even greater when things seem to be at
your beck and call.
Through it all, whether it be just an ordinary day,
Put all you can into it, the beauty will come as you watch it pay.

An Unusual Day

A most unusual day it is, with its very, very dreary look.
Some dark skies hoover overhead as I sit writing in this book.
The weatherman says it just might rain, showering from east to west.
As I looked out of my window, the thought comes that God knows best.

He gives us sunshine and rain.
It's through the Master comes our golden grain.
Who are we to sit idly around and judge,
What weather we should have, let's not hold a grudge.

Did you ever stop to think what life would be but like,
If the weather changes, we go on a strike?
Without the rain, without the sun,
Without spring, summer, fall, and winter, there'd be no fun.

God gave this life and world meaning, He made it for us all.
The moon the stars, day and night are at His beck and call.
Now these things let us know and constantly keeps us aware.
A supreme being made this world possible because of His loving tender care.

December 30, 1986

A Rainy Day

Storm clouds have gathered and all is dark and gray.
The weatherman has forecast it'll be a rainy day.
Plans to go shopping or visiting must all be put aside.
Neither can you go walking or go for a nice long ride.

The raindrops have started to come down very fast.
There are so many people who hope this storm won't last.
Schoolchildren and workers all over the town,
May have to come home as the rain pours down.

Faster and faster the rain seems to drop.
Falling on trees and every rooftop.
It gathers momentum as it falls from the sky.
The ground is so wet it'll take some time to dry.

It could be snow, rather than rain.
Of that we can be thankful, snow can cause much pain.
The rain is needed to make the plants and flowers grow.
The grass becomes greener lending beauty to nature's picturesque show.

Without rain, there'd be no water to drink,
This rain is refreshing, don't you think?
It fills the rivers, oceans, and the sea,
Making this earth a better place for you and me.

Friday, February 12, 1988

Rain, Rain, Rain

Rain, rain, rain, that's what it's all about.
I'm sure all of the farmers could just jump up and shout.
Many have become discouraged because of the drought.
Much of their crops and stock no longer can be brought.

Hurricanes have taken a great big toll everywhere.
Floods can be seen with tides gushing and rising through towns and cities, making them almost bare.
The work of God never ceases, His supremacy is always there.
These things let you know His great works are beyond compare.

Rain made this air much cooler and the grass much greener too.
It gave the earth a much cleaner smell, making it much healthier for me and you.
Now let us all be thankful that God has brought this rain about.
Without the rain we're having we just might be stuck with that drought.

A Summer Night

As I lie quietly in my little bed,
All kinds of thoughts run through my head.
My room is dark, and I can't see,
The many objects that are all around me.

The fresh air blows through my open windows,
Bending the tall trees that can be seen in the dark shadows.
A summer night and all is so still,
Quiet and peaceful as I rest here and thrill.

To be able to rest here and be content,
Is a blessing from heaven and surely godsent,
Just to know no evil is lurking in the dark,
Your fears and worries will no longer stark.

As I lie in my bed all noise is gone.
My eyes grow heavy and sleep comes on.
I can no longer stay awake.
This will be the end until daybreak.

The Benefits of Weather

When you see a rainbow, peeping down from the sky,
It's there to tell you the sky will no longer cry.
The sun is on its way to give you a thrill.
It'll pierce your soul making you happy and helping you uphill.

God makes the weather all through the year.
If it weren't for its many changes we'd have quite a bit to fear.
Sunshine and rain bring the harvest, grain, and our daily food.
These are the things we need to survive and keep us in a good mood.

So let us all be thankful for these wonders from above.
God is just showering us with His blessings and continuing to give us love.
So when the weatherman tells us it's going to be a rainy or sunny day,
Enjoy that day to the fullest, it's God's work paving your way.

May 1, 1987

A Windy Night

Did you hear that wind last night,
Howling and whistling in its maddening plight,
Frightening sounds that seem to say,
Boooo, boooo, clatter clatter, get out of my way.

The house seemed to shake as the wind passed by,
Noisy and blowing against the roof so high.
The windows rattled and shook seeming to speak,
As if they knew the wind was at its very peak.

Is seemed to be telling a tale of woe,
As if calling out for help against a dreadful foe.
Faster and faster it picked up speed,
Chanting sounds and cries most unusual indeed.

The wind continued to sing its very sad song,
As if to be saying someone had done it wrong.
It blew and blew as the night went past,
Constantly giving out its terrible blast.

It screeched and groaned giving a high-pitched tune,
Making you wish you weren't home alone.
Subside it wouldn't as the night went by,
The wind almost making you want to cry.

Finally, the wind suddenly ceased to blow and gradually came to a halt.
It quieted down with nothing seeming to be at fault,
A night to remember as the wind passed through,
Leaving you shaking, not knowing what to do.

February 8, 1988

A Hot Day

Not a sign of a breeze anywhere,
The sun is beaming very hot rays out there.
It burns the grass and leaves on the trees.
Everyone outside is ill at ease.

The sidewalk is so hot it could fry an egg.
Folks outside are mostly exposing their legs.
Some cover up in pants and jeans.
Long skirts are back in style, it seems.

It is a very hot August day.
There's probably no relief on the way.
How to survive in weather like this,
Is the chief concern of all who are amidst.

The best bet of all is to remain at home,
There you can see TV and talk on the phone.
Keep cool with your fan or central air.
At all times look out for your own welfare.

August 1987

Flowers Make for Beauty

Flowers are magnificent and best known for their beauty.
They're great to behold, spreading fragrance is usually their duty.
Most times they are sent to ones you love very, very dear.
Whatever the occasion, they'll bring an abundance of cheer.

Flowers in the home scattered about,
Whether real or artificial, lend beauty inside or out.
When one wants to create an air of romance,
Beautiful flower arrangements will definitely enhance.

Now flowers are definitely great to behold.
Plant them as you buy them and watch them unfold,
Beauty the likes of which some have never seen,
When you walk in their midst you feel as if in a dream.

When years creep on you, and you began to get old,
Flowers keep you company, so I'm told.
So put in your life as many flowers as you can.
They bring happiness, contentment, and joy to your daily plan.

October 20, 1986

Wisdom on a Rainy Day

Rain and ice are here today,
Making it slippery all the way.
Icicles hanging from the tall trees above,
Shining and fitting the branches like a glove.

Shadows seem to form in the far distant sky,
Making the earth dark, I know not why.
Window panes glisten with icy beads,
Dancing and melting with a great deal of speed.

See them pitter-patter as they constantly fall,
Here, there, and yonder in many a tiny ball.
Oh, what a beautiful sight to see,
The icy rain singing a song for you and me.

The rain made the roads slick, they look like glass,
Cars are slipping afraid to pass.
Unsafe to drive, unsafe to walk,
One could become a statistic that no longer can talk.

So be careful, on a day like this, just rest,
Enjoy your home, looking out the window would be best,
Be wise on a rainy day,
Stay inside and watch the weather at play.

January 4, 1985

The Beauty of a Tree

Trees are like people standing tall,
Waving their arms in a beckoning call.
Bowing their heads as if to speak,
Seeming very great, yet humble and meek.

Trees are a beautiful sight to behold,
Some stretching up to the sky looking so bold.
Yet, some are short and medium in height,
Making a glorious border in the sky so bright.

In autumn, their leaves turn yellow and gold.
It's surprising to see the sight they unfold.
Brown, red, and purple and so many hues.
Lend to their beauty and foliage too.

Later they become very, very bare,
Making it possible for the seasons to compare.
Their shedding is such a great mystic treat,
Proving *Mother Nature* just can't be beat.

When spring comes around, they all turn green.
The bare limbs blossoming can clearly be seen.
Now this is surely a beautiful sight.
When spring announces its most unusual plight.

New Year

A Brand-new Year

The year goes out full of memories, some good and some bad.
But most of all we must give thanks, and look to heaven and be glad.
We've lived to greet a brand-new year.
Many didn't make it; some we hold so dear.

Give thanks and praise the Father above,
Who always has showered us with His constant love.
Kneel down and pray as the year comes in,
With His blessings and guidance, you'll always win.

A new year founded on faith in God,
Will reap you a year of happiness as you onward plod.
Step out to accomplish your aims and goals,
God will make two steps for each one of yours, as the year unfolds.

Greeting a New Year

Christmas has gone the lights have faded away.
You are ready to start a brand-new day.
It was nice while it lasted with its cheery mood.
Frolicking and feasting on all kinds of food.

But you must get ready for the oncoming year,
Face all its problems and be ready to cheer,
The birth of the New Year as it comes into sight,
And plan to make all its days shiny and bright.

Resolutions are in order to get a new start.
Stick to them always and from them never part.
Be kind to your brother should be a rule.
Love one another that's being very cool.

Give thanks to God daily for all He has done.
For this He'll bless you, then your battle will be won.
Push onward and upward with all your might.
To be a success in this New Year you must constantly fight.

Ask God to guide you and show you the way.
To find happiness and love in this godforsaken day.
You must have peace with yourself and also man.
Plan a future with your family, give them a hand.

Greeting a New Year (Cont'd)

Now as you step out into new fields of endeavor,
Keep an open mind so you can weather,
All changes that take place here or worldwide,
Meeting them with a challenge and ending up with pride.

Pride in yourself and a job well done,
Faith to continue until the battle is won.
Now as you journey in the New Year from day to day,
Don't ever forget to thank God and pray.

After-Christmas Thoughts

Christmas has come and gone.
Did you get its true meaning? A Christ Child was born.
Was there only a feeling for meaningless things?
Like toys, lights, trees, and the gifts Christmas brings?

The Christ Child was born to bring peace and joy to this earth.
We celebrate Christmas because that's the day of His birth.
Born in a manger with nothing but hay,
He came to this earth to brighten our day.

What did you do to bring joy to others?
The homeless, the poor, and the sick are our brothers.
They need your love and constant care.
As the year comes in, let's be more aware.

As Christians and in a country of very great wealth,
Plans should be made to shelter, feed, and keep the poor in good health.
The meaning of Christmas should always be there,
Since the Christ Child was born to teach us to share.

Let the new year be bright and good to us all.
God bless us and keep us that our country won't fall.
Show us the way to bring peace and joy to all mankind.
Let thy love prevail that the nations are blessed and the world they'll
never destroy, giving us all Peace of mind.

December 30, 1986

A Brand-new Year

A brand-new year, why not start off right?
A brand-new year, what a wonderful plight?
To put behind all the things that were wrong.
And plunge into your future, with a gladdening song.

A brand-new year, making beautiful dreams,
Not just things hoped for, but things that are real and make you beam.
Off to a fresh start, accomplishing those things,
Placed in the background and years never seem to bring.

Get on with your life and make those things happen each day.
That are beautiful to you and beneficial as you pass this way.
Venture out into the new paths and channels you meet.
Greet them with a smile and challenge; you will conquer and not have defeat.

Labor on in that grand upward way.
Your dreams will come true, their fulfillment will pay.
A brand-new year, started off just right.
With a will to conquer and continue to fight.

December 30, 1986

Looking Toward the Future

What are your plans for the upcoming year?
Do you look into the future and feel fear?
What does the future hold for me?
Is it success or failure, why can't we see?

Man cannot predict his oncoming fate,
His life can't be measured at any rate,
Although he puts all he possesses into each and every task every day,
Something oft goes wrong that he didn't expect, causing a delay.

He mustn't give up, he must continue to wage the fight,
Continue the battle each day and night.
Find new ideas and ways to help the cause along,
Then put them into use they might not be wrong.

Yes, one does not know what the New Year will bring.
Always think positively, it's the best thing.
You can make things possible; if you only but try,
Life can be beautiful as the years go by.

December 30, 1986

Pets

Dedicated to My Kitten

Mother's Day Gift

A black and white kitten is a beautiful pet,
Or maybe any kind of kitten that you can get.
They bring joy to you as you watch them play,
They get lazier and lazier every day.

What fun it is to see them frolic about,
Nibbling and tearing at anything that's out.
Jumping and running all around your feet,
Letting you know he's ready for a treat.

His day is made up mostly of play,
It seems he never wants to hit the hay.
But sooner or later he tires out?
Curls up in a knot forgetting what it's all about.

Dogs

A doggie is a nice thing to have around,
He's known as man's best friend in every town.
He follows you from place to place,
His love and affections know no race.

They alarm the neighborhood as prowlers pass,
Wanting you to watch out a burglar could be lurking in the grass.
He barks and barks to let you know,
Someone is out there, you better go slow.

He is lovable and sweet.
Smelling everyone and thing he meets.
He's a valuable asset to all mankind,
A friend indeed to ease your mind.

Prayers

Prayer Is the Answer

Did you say your prayers today?
Thank God in your very own way,
For the kind and noble things,
That His blessings always brings.

Have you asked for forgiveness too?
Are your prayers way overdue?
Have you talked with God today?
Did you forget to get down on your knees and pray?

Why carry all that heavy load around,
When you can leave it with God and not let it get you down.
Prayer is the answer, so just have faith today.
In His own time, He'll show you the way.

He knows just how much you can bear.
His plans for you are always dealt out fair.
So be thankful for the little things as days and years go past.
He'll award you with greater things that will last and last.

October 20, 1986

A Solemn Sincere Prayer

Oh, God, please unite us as we pass this way.
Continue to strengthen us from day to day.
Give us faith and fortitude, also courage that we can withstand,
The constant trials and tribulations forever present and on hand.

Guide us and direct us as we forge ahead,
In the paths of life that we walk daily and tread
Teach us to live as Thou wouldst have us to,
So that we may be more holy and closer to You.

Lift our spirits high, as we go forward each and every day.
Aid us to meet the challenges that constantly come our way.
Send us the so-needed warmth, comfort, and love,
Of family, friends, and neighbors, and Yours from above.

We're thankful for Your many blessings and protection and want You
to know,
We are forever grateful, for we needed them to grow.
For clothing, shelter, and constant daily bread,
To You, we give thanks that we've always been blessed and fed.

You know our every weakness and also many sins.
Forgive us, Father, help us not to make them over again.
Make us humble and meek, as we continue to journey on.
That we may be always mindful of what's right and also wrong.

Give us the wisdom and foresight that we may always see,
Dangers that lurk in the shadows of this life to be.
Reach out and touch our hearts, dear God.
Make our thoughts pure and filled with Thy love.

A Solemn Sincere Prayer (Cont'd)

Show us the way that Thou wouldst have us go.
Make us more useful and help the world to grow.
Bless all Your dear children on this vast enormous earth.
They too need Your help from the time of their birth.

Bless the sick and afflicted, they too need You so,
Clothe all in their right minds, so they too might have a chance to grow.
Fruitful and wise and find a place in this life,
And build a tomorrow that's not full of strife.

Now, God, You have heard our humble plea,
Make us the kind of people You want us to be.
Take away all sin and temptations that pass our way.
Forgive us for all our wrongdoings we humbly pray.

Help us strive to live more devoted to thee,
Close and closer, let us grow is our plea.
Endow us with wisdom from Your holy book,
That we may better understand the sacrifice You took.

Let us grow in grace and power and become stronger through You.
That our lives on this earth may become more dedicated too.
May we reach out to help the unfortunate, as we pass along.
Bless us all, dear God, that the entire world will become united and
strong.

A Prayer of Thanks

As I say my prayers at night,
I thank God with all my might,
For His many blessings kind and true,
Tender loving care, mercy, and guidance too.

Through each daily task and chore,
You light up the way that I may score.
In all the jobs I must perform,
At school, at church, at play, and home.

I thank You, God, for my family too,
Friends and relatives and neighbors who,
You've blessed and blessed each and every day,
In Your own very special kind of way.

You know my wants and daily needs.
I thank You, God, these things You did heed.
You've blessed me once, You've blessed me thrice.
You've been to me everything so very nice.

How can I ever repay
The tremendous debt I owe to You this day?
Please help me as I go along,
To gain more faith and to thee be strong.

Help me, dear God, to walk with thee,
So life can be beautiful, clean, and free,
From sin, sorrow, woes, and strife,
That confront us daily as we walk in this life.

God Answers Prayer

If you were meant by God to be,
Different from others, though the whole world may not see.
He knows your mind, heart, aims, ambitions, and goals.
He knows the thoughts you carry deeply rooted down in your soul.

He hears your prayers from day to day,
Though things never seem to be going your way.
Always remember and keep this thought in mind,
God always answers prayer in due time.

Life's Struggles for Happiness

To always be happy would be a wonderful thing,
But one must learn to deal with what life may bring.
Sometimes you are dealt a terrible blow,
Oft times from fellowmen you do not know.
Deeds of unkindness as years go by,
You don't care to seem weak but wish to cry and cry.
You only have left just a little bit of will,
To keep on pushing and climbing up that hill.
To give up surely would be a very sad mistake.
'Cause all your enemies are just watching and waiting for you to break.
So you get to your knees and pray to God,
To show you the path that you should trod.
To make all these knots that have come your way,
Be kicks forward to brighten your day.

April 20, 1984

Seasons

A Late Spring

It's still cold, and it looks a little bit wintry,
Rainy and wet, it seems like a century.
Storm clouds gather in the passing night,
It's supposed to be springtime, and days should be bright.

Flowers are blooming, saying spring is here,
Yet old man winter seemingly won't disappear.
Passing winds howl and blow through the trees,
Let's hope tomorrow won't be a deep freeze.

Please, Mr. Winter, just go away.
Give springtime a chance to come out and play.
She's such a beautiful season,
What you are doing is just not in reason.

Spring enhances the earth and just makes it glow.
Its warmth should pierce the air and make things grow.
Go away, winter, your time is past.
Can't you tell it's not your season, see the pretty green grass?

Now, Mr. Winter, you've stayed too long.
Birds in the treetops are singing that song.
They too, wish you would go away.
Come back in your season, and let them frolic and play.

Oh, springtime, you can't be too far behind,
With trees budding and birds singing songs that rhyme.
You are indeed a great delight.
Please hurry, wind your way to make things bright.

April 30, 1987

Fall

Fall is a beautiful time of year.
It's as pretty as the springtime that we hold so dear.
It's this brisk air and gentle blowing wind.
Quickens your breath, saying I am a friend.

The leaves fall down from the trees you pass,
Littering the walks, path, and grass.
What beautiful colors are there to see,
Making the world bright for you and me.

Autumn days are surely godsent.
They let you know some changes are meant,
To give you a different kind of view,
Telling us life can be just as beautiful too.

A Windy Night

Did you hear that wind last night,
Howling and whistling in its maddening plight?
Frightening sounds that seemed to say.
Boooo, boooo. Clatter, clatter, get out of my way.

The house seemed to shake as the wind passed by,
Noisy and blowing against the roof so high.
The windows rattled and shook seeming to speak,
As if they knew the wind was at its very peak.

It seemed to be telling a tale of woe,
As if calling out for help against a dreadful foe.
Faster and faster it picked up speed,
Chanting sounds and cries most unusual indeed.

The wind continued to sing its very sad song.
As if to be saying someone has done it wrong.
It blew and blew as the night went past,
Constantly giving out its terrible blast.

It screeched and groaned giving a high-pitched tone,
Making you wish you weren't home alone.
Subdue it wouldn't as the night went by,
The wind almost making you want to cry.

Finally the wind ceased to blow and gradually came to a halt.
They quieted down, nothing seemed to be at fault.
A night to remember as the wind passed through,
Leaving you shaking not knowing what to do.

February 8, 1988

An Autumn Day

Fall is a beautiful time and season in the year,
With its spectacular scenery that we hold so dear.
Nothing is more divine than a great autumn day,
With light winds blowing the tree branches, causing them to sway.

Leaves of bright red, orange, purple, yellow, and gold,
Fall from the treetops in a fashion untold.
They flutter about on the ground, paths, and walks,
Some are so dried and crisp, they almost seem to talk.

That pungent air is so fresh and sends out a smell of delight,
You have a pleasurable feeling making the day seem bright.
A feeling of peace and contentment grows within yourself,
Dismantling disbelief and placing fears and doubts on the shelf.

Your hopes become alive, and you're grateful too,
That you can enjoy a day like this through and through.
Your thoughts turn to God because He is the one,
Who made a day like this possible and embodied with much fun.

October 16, 1986

Winter Is Here

The sun came out right after the snow.
It gave the snow a terrible blow.
It melted it down bit by bit,
Oh, the sun gave that snow quite a fit!

Only small segments can now be seen.
The icy road is now very, very clear.
The cars can drive safely to and fro,
Neighbors and friends can travel wherever they wish to go.

Who would have thought it would go so fast?
Usually, it comes and lasts and lasts.
This time it brought a message clear.
Letting you know old man winter is here.

January 5, 1985

Spring

Do you ever stop and stare
Up in the treetops where they're bare?
Then in the spring see them budding out,
And begin to wonder what nature is all about?

It's spring, the most wonderful season of the year,
Spreading beauty and sunshine so it won't be drear.
It's letting you know God's not dead,
He's making the earth more beautiful for us to tread.

The sky is blue as blue can be,
Covering the earth, woods, and sea.
What a tremendous sight to behold,
Colorful masks of foliage, brown, purple, green, and gold.

Yes, birds can be heard chirping their songs
Making melodious tunes as they go along.
Rabbits and squirrels hop here and there,
Black, brown, and white can be seen everywhere.

The ground has become a carpet of green.
Its beauty is like something you've never seen.
Flowers have scented their fragrant air.
Making the breezes smell sweet everywhere.

Spring (Cont'd)

God gives us spring to help us smile,
To let you know living is still worthwhile.
It is spring when we're usually at our best,
In work and play and all the rest.

Enjoy it while the season lasts,
Get out in the open, don't let it pass.
Do something you've always wanted to,
This spring weather was put here for you and you.

April 8, 1986

Winter Weather

The weather outside is very, very cold.
It's almost 30 degrees, so I am told.
You stay inside trying to keep warm.
The chill gets to your feet doing its harm.

You turn up the heater to warm your toes.
It's a slow process when the feeling goes.
Finally, you begin to thaw just a little.
What a relief that brings as your toes twiddle.

The weatherman says it just might snow.
I certainly hope he's mistaken and does not know.
Snow is something to look at for beauty:
But cleaning it up is a mess, and your solemn duty.

Oh, well, it's winter what do you expect.
Without the snow, germs would collect and collect.
Nature has its own way of keeping us from hurt harm and danger.
So let's just be thankful so to Him who was born in a manger.

The Splendors of Spring

Budding flowers everywhere, Spring is on its way,
Daffodils, jonquils, and tulips make a colorful display.
They're flowering and spreading their fragrance in midair,
And making beautiful borders here and there.

Spring is a fun time, don't you agree?
All Nature parades for everyone to see.
Birds flutter about singing melodious songs so sweet.
Rabbits and squirrels run and hop, dashing across the street.

Children play in babbling brooks and streams,
Splashing and wading as their little faces and countenance gleams.
Many are gathered in groups here and there,
Engaging in tennis, softball, or baseball with teams or in a pair.

Visions of Spring have caught everyone's eye.
It can truthfully be said, Spring has kissed old man Winter goodbye.
The air is warm and sweet as you step outside.
You glance at Spring's beauty with a great warmth inside.

Spring, 1988

Autumn Leaves

Yellow, red, purple, and brown,
These are the colors of the leaves coming down.
Falling and scattering everywhere,
Making stacks and heaps, here and there.

Noisily they crunch as you walk along,
Oft time seemingly singing a song.
Rustling, moving hither and there.
You look around they are everywhere.

Autumn you are a season of beauty and grandeur,
Coloring the countryside, cities and woodlands are a wonder.
Your brisk air fills the soul of man,
Who walks and breathes the fragrances you expand.

What earthly beauty do you possess?
Words can't convey the charm of your caress.
Your colorful hues are seen from the treetops.
You brighten the world, so please don't stop.

Beautiful Month of May

May is here today with its bright sunshine.
It is a beautiful month so warm and fine.
Flowers are gradually appearing over hill and dale.
Squirrels are finally coming out, wagging their bushy tails.

Birds chirp loudly in the treetops, singing all day long.
You wonder what they are saying as they chirp their melodious song.
Finally, they venture down and land on your nice green grass.
Their colors and feathers are so beautiful when they go pass.

April showers brought the flowers, that we enjoy in May.
May, you came in splendor and your beauty is here to stay.
The air is filled with your fragrance, a delight to breathe and smell.
Is this your way of telling us that all is well?

The Oncoming Spring

The snow has gone, the sun is out,
Of course, most people would like to shout.
Come, Spring, we know you're on your way.
Hurry, hurry, please don't let ole Winter stay.

Spring you're the most beautiful season of them all.
Next to you, I'd say it's beautiful Fall.
Now the trees are trying to bud as you can see,
They are bending and nodding their heads at me.

They're happy to welcome the oncoming Spring,
With its lovely flowers and everything.
Earth is dressed and robed in dazzling green,
The likes of which some have never seen.

Spring is approaching, can't you tell?
Truly it can be recognized by its melodious smell.
Sweet jonquils, tulips, and forsythia bright,
Are sending out a fragrance of great delight.

Kites are flying high in the sky so blue.
Children are underneath making a dream come true.
Others sail their tiny little ships,
In small puddles made as the rain drips and drips.

Many wade in the nearby babbling brook.
Yes, Spring is here, just take a look.
Oh, Spring how glad we are to welcome you.
You make us all happy, through and through.

February 15, 1985

The Beauty of Fall

The wind blows gently through the trees.
The branches and leaves are bending and rustling in the breeze,
Autumn and its beauty are approaching fast each day.
You can see and feel it in the air as the branches sway.

Yellow, purple, brown, red, and gold,
These colors are seen more and more as fall unfolds.
A sight to behold as you saunter around,
Fall is spreading its beauty from town to town.

Seasons come and seasons go.
Fall is more picturesque as it puts on its show.
It is decked out and dressed up for all of us to see.
The wonders of nature that God made for you and me.

October 1, 1988

Rain Brings Spring

It's a cloudy day with no sun in the sky.
Dark clouds are not visible, yet the sky just might cry.
April rains now shower in March this year.
That's a little unusual and somewhat queer.

An early spring has been predicted by all.
I'm sure it will be welcomed and nice to hear the bird's mating call.
It'll be a pleasure to see the tulips, violets, dogwood, jonquils, and
    forsythia bloom.
All earth will become green and beautiful, casting away all gloom.

Coats, boots, and sweaters can be cast aside.
The air will become warmer, then you'll enjoy going outside.
A ride in the country will be a nice delight.
A picnic or a swim at the beach will be just right.

Mother Nature is such a wonderful thing.
As the seasons come and go, it's a pleasure to see what nature will bring.
It so happens that God made it possible for us to see,
Earth's colorful changes as He would have them be.

March 10, 1988

Welcome Spring

Trees are gradually budding all around,
As the March wind whistles and utters a cheery sound.
Woo, woo, woo, Spring is on the way.
Soon dear children you may come out and play.

The birds can be heard as they sing and chirp very gaily.
They sit high in the treetops and move about daily.
Sparrows, blackbirds, robins, and crows,
Can be seen up in the branches as they wave and sway to and fro.

The sky is oft lit with a glowing hew.
We may see up there sometimes a rainbow too.
Longer and longer becomes each day,
Greeting Spring in its formal way

The sleeping flowers will soon awake,
Adding beauty and fragrance to earth and lake.
Oh, Spring, you are such a wonderful sight,
To all the world you are a great delight.

About the Author

Beatrice Wilson Crutchfield, born on June 20, 1913, was a native of Newport News, VA. She was the youngest of four children.

She received her bachelor of science degree, in secondary education, from Virginia State College. There she became a member of Alpha Kappa Alpha Sorority, Inc., in 1931. She also attended Wilson Salem College where she changed her major to early education and studied music and choir directing under the famous Noah Rider. She furthered her education at Hampton Institute and DC Teachers College in Washington, D.C.

Her teaching career started at John Marshall School, Newport News, Virginia, where she began elementary training. She retired from Smothers Elementary School in 1983, after twenty-five years of educational service. During her retirement celebration, teachers and former students expressed their appreciation for her dedication.

Among her many awards, she received that of Business Woman of the Year for ownership and operation of a Women's Apparel Shop in Newport News, Virginia. In addition, she was honored as woman of the year by the Business Woman's Sorority of Tidewater Virginia.

She was a charter member of the Jack and Jill of America, in Newport News. She served in many capacities at First Baptist Church, was actively involved with Lambert Omega Chapter of Alpha Kappa Alpha Sorority, Inc., served as president of the Quettes and was a member of the Continentals.

On September 2, 1937, she married the late Rucker C. Crutchfield, Jr. She was the loving mother of Loreathea A. Fields, Silvia M. Daniels and Rucker C. Crutchfield III. Her sons-in-law were the late William D. Fields, Sr. and the late Joseph D. Daniels.

Her daughter-in-law was Carol Johnson Dean. She was the proud grandmother of William D. Fields, Jr., Dana M. Daniels,

Cicily D. Daniels Macias, and Rucker C. Johnson. Her great grandchildren are Summer Joy C. Fields, William D. Fields III, Rucker C. Johnson, Jr., Lalah Johnson, and Celina Elise Macias.

While in Washington, D.C., she was a member of Brookland Union Baptist Church where she sang in the choir, actively participated in the June Club, worked in the Sunday School and served on the education committee. She was an active member of Xi Sigma Omega Chapter of Alpha Kappa Alpha Sorority, Inc., in Upper Montgomery County, Maryland. As a Golden Soror, she served many years of her gifts and talents in Alpha Kappa Alpha Sorority, Inc. As a result of her service, Xi Sigma Omega Chapter arranged to publish her first book of poetry on October 21, 2001.

She has a collection of other poetry and tributes to members of Brookland Union Baptist Church and the sorority, which are being published separately.

She enjoyed the fellowship of church members, neighbors, and friends. She had a tremendous zest for living and enjoyed traveling with her family.

She was a talented, prolific writer of poetry and was always willing to share her gifts with anyone who asked.

Printed in the USA
CPSIA information can be obtained
at www.ICGtesting.com
CBHW030942130324
5310CB00001B/4